To Kri,

From
Robyn HChoh Nov 17 2021

American as Apple Pie

AN AUTOBIOGRAPHY

RODNEY H. CHOW

AMERICAN AS APPLE PIE

AN AUTOBIOGRAPHY

© 2021, Rodney H. Chow.

Print ISBN: 978-1-09837-6-697

eBook ISBN: 978-1-09837-6-703

CONTENTS

GETTING YOU
TO KNOW ME

One Sunday, I got bored. So, I drove to Los Angeles Chinatown and stopped in at my favorite hole-in-the wall greasy spoon. Some people might not be brave enough to eat there because it doesn't look like a well-run eating place. But locals don't mind. They do not care how the dining area looks as long as the food is great. As usual, a long line of customers stood patiently waiting to buy those delicious dim sums. My turn came. I said politely in Chinese: "*Please place my order in a box, not in a bag.*" I saw everyone else's orders placed in Styrofoam box and all boxes placed in bags. I wanted mine in a Styrofoam box inside a large box. A box would be safer in my car for the long drive home.

But this is Back-Woodsville. Opinions are direct. Who would waste time with courtesy? Customers have been standing in line waiting to buy. There is no time to waste. The sales lady said to me with her go-to-hell attitude, "*You are Chinese! Otherwise, I would not put those (Styrofoam containers) in a bag for you.*" She took my money, handed the bag to me, turned to the person behind me, and said, "*Next*"

What??? Every customer had their purchases placed in containers and carried them in a bag. She spoke to me as if I was being treated special. Oh well!!! I have been living in Politesville too long. I had just momentarily relived my down-to-earth days among peasants.

What the hell! They are my people! I love them.

PROLOGUE

People sometimes ask me, ***"When did you arrive here?"*** I thought it was obvious that although I grew up in a neighborhood of recent arrivals, I am not first generation. I am fifth generation American.

My maternal grandfather's great grandfather landed in Oregon sometime around the year 1812. He later returned to China and had a son. In around the 1860's, his son came to California and became a laborer building the Central Pacific Railroad across the Sierra Nevada Mountains in Northern California. He was a member of the black powder gang that blasted away the granite mountainside at Cape Horn near the Town of Colfax. He was my Grandfather's father. Eventually, that side of our family tree settled in San Francisco. My paternal grandfather was a farm laborer in the pineapple fields in Hawaii. Pop left Hawaii in his early 20's and went to Locke, in the Sacramento Delta, a town built by Chinese immigrants in the early 20th century. He chose that town because they were his kinfolks, the *CHUNG SAAN* dialect speaking people. Most of them were from the same village in China.

Even though I have often mentioned this portion of my family history, some Caucasians do not picture me as a typical American, although my family has been in California for almost 200 years.

Upon hearing that, someone once said to me.

You are more American than most of us.

That's not what I wanted to hear. I wanted something more meaningful, like walking down the street and being seen as someone who BELONGS. There is so much about me I want everyone to understand. So, I decided to write my autobiography.

INTRODUCTION

I t took a major portion of my life to learn the goodness in others who were different than me. The most important challenge was overcoming pitfalls and hard feelings. Then I realized unity is possible if we are willing to concentrate on the good in each other instead of focusing on the bad.

This story is about my journey in reaching this goal. It is about my life from as early as I can remember, including what I heard from my elders.

Although I was born American, ***it took a lifetime for me to become one.***

Come; join me on my journey to becoming fully American.

CHAPTER 1
THE BEGINNING OF MY STORY

Pop farmed 80 acres of Bartlett pears in the Sacramento delta during the late nineteen twenties near the town of Locke. He was a sharecropper. Although our family started there, my story begins in Los Angeles after Pop lost everything at the beginning of the Great Depression. The time when he had to start over from rock bottom. Our first home was in Old Chinatown on Alameda Street, Los Angeles, California where the Railroad Union Station now exists.

It is here, in old Chinatown, in the year 1930, where my life story starts. When Pop took whatever job, he could find and became a dishwasher in a Chinese restaurant. It was within walking distant from our apartment, and he didn't mind doing such menial work. It provided an income, enough to pay the rent and buy food for us (Pop, Mom, my sister Prudy and I). However, being a laborer was not his cup of tea. He carefully saved as much money as possible, to some day, buy a used panel truck. He had visions of becoming a fish peddler selling to the Chinese community.

Pop told me that when he arrived in Los Angeles, all the apartments in old Chinatown were taken, except for one upstairs unit there. It had been vacant for a long time. He took it immediately and sent for us to come join him. Not too long afterward, he found a better less crowded place, on San Julian Street. As we were moving out, the Chinese neighbors stood around us and stared. That bothered him.

Why are you staring at me like that? he asked.

One person spoke up. *How you like that apartment?*

Pop didn't think that was an unusual question, so he replied.

We were very comfortable. We like it. Why do you ask?

Someone was murdered there; his ghost is haunting it, he replied.

As Pop was telling me this story, he faced me, chuckled and said:

I think it was because we were so poor that the ghost felt sorry for us and left us alone.

After several moves, we settled on 21st Street. I remember vividly what happened in 1934, when I walked home from Kindergarten.

Screech! Drivers slammed on their brakes and skidded to a stop.

Honk! Honk! Honk! Horns blared as the cars desperately tried not to hit me. I was just five years old, walking nonchalantly across Central Avenue, too young to realize the danger of being run over by cars. Mom had instructed me to use the tunnel instead of that busy street.

But that tunnel was a toilet for the homeless. The floor was covered with feces, and the stench was awful. Just a few days before, while walking through the tunnel, I slipped and fell. You should have seen Mom's face when I walked through the door. She immediately washed me down, then dressed me in clean clothes, but still insisted I use the tunnel. I was not going to walk through that awful place again. Instead, I walked across the street amid all the traffic. Mom was not aware I was disobeying her instructions.

As I approached the curb, there stood this man. I recognized him. He sold newspapers and magazines in his store. He saw the whole episode, and boy was he mad! He stared at me, grabbed my arm, and loudly scolded me.

Don't you cross the street like that again!

He told Mom what happened, so here came the second round of scolding and lectures. Mom was very upset with me.

Why didn't you use the tunnel? You could have been hit by a car.

I looked up at her and said the only thing on my mind.

That man is mean.

Later, Mom told everyone how upset she was, not because I did not follow her instructions, but because the only thing that bothered me was how that man had scolded me. I learned nothing from that experience.

Crossing streets was just routine for going to and from school. But when the Kindergarten teacher took us to see the school garden, that was something new. We walked single file to a fence that had a board missing. We stepped through the opening and saw a yard full of blooming flowers. I had never seen anything so beautiful.

During playtime in Kindergarten, I hesitated to play with the children in my class. Before I went to school, my playmates and everyone around me were part of my family or the Wong family from across the alley. The children in Kindergarten looked very different from those I knew. The teacher spoke to Mom.

Why is Rodney not playing with the other children? she asked.

Rodney doesn't know how to play with Black children. He has to learn to mix with others different than his own kind, Mom said.

RODNEY ONE-YEAR-OLD
1010 Stockton Street, San Francisco, California
Notations in Chinese on the right are the date photo was taken and my Chinese name "GING FEE." Translated, I think it means "PACER."

CHAPTER 2
DISCOVERING LIFE AS
A FOUR-YEAR-OLD CHILD

I watched Uncle Joe throw overripe tomatoes onto the fence, showing off to me like a typical teenager. He stopped for a moment, turned towards me and said:

This is how I plant tomatoes.

I believed every word.

Another time, someone said that the small tree in front of our house was an orange tree. So, every day, I went out to look at it, hoping to find an orange. Some of the leaves were curled because of insect damage, but I didn't know that; I thought it was the beginning of a fruit. Finally, days later, I lost interest.

I made a new discovery. Pop's fish truck! It was parked in the garage. Gosh, if I pressed this thing sticking out from the tires, it made a hissing sound. I kept on pressing it, just to hear that sound. Then it stopped.

The next morning, Pop started to take out his truck to go peddling fish. One of his tires was flat. He had to use valuable time to change it. Well, you know what happened. Another scolding and lecture from Mom.

Pop brought home sacks of walnuts from the wholesale nut market. They paid him for each sack shelled. So, Mom sat me, my sisters and brother together around the table and made a game shelling the walnuts. She told us how to use a hammer to crack them open. Then she said:

Let's see who can take out the most walnuts without breaking them into pieces.

I loved the game. Each time I took out a perfect one, I shouted:

I got a whole one! I didn't break it in pieces.

I had so much fun trying to do better than my sister,
Pop scattered the shells on the dirt driveway to keep the dust down, and it became my hunting grounds for perfect half shells to use as toy boats.

My favorite toy was a yellow teddy bear. It never left my side. It was my constant companion. One day, I looked and looked but couldn't find it. After several days of searching, I gave up looking. Years later, Mom mentioned how filthy it was from all the dirt accumulated on it. She just threw it away. She did not realize how much that toy meant to me.

One Sunday, Pop, my uncles, Mom, my brother and my sisters were outside on our yard. I enjoyed that time so much. It made me so happy just being with everyone on the grassy lawn in front of our home. It was such a nice day. and Uncle John thought it would be nice for all of us to just go outside instead of staying in the house. Uncle John took photos of us. We weren't doing anything special. The whole family was just outside enjoying each other on a sunny afternoon. Those are the days I relive with nostalgia today.

A more serious event occurred while we were living on 21st Street. I saw Mom spreading newspaper on top of her mattress. Then Uncle John took us into the kitchen and closed the door. I still remember hearing the footsteps of people coming in and out of the house. Then Pop came in. He handed each of us a piece of candy and told us to eat it. I didn't realize it then. Pop needed something to lighten up his spirit. This was his way to lighten up the situation. He had called the emergency hospital for help, and the ambulance came to take Mom to the hospital.

The next few days, Uncle John took care of us so Pop could continue peddling fish. Several days went by. Then Mom came home. I had a new bother.

Many years later, I learned that Mom had planned on having the baby at home with no medical help. Pop could not afford a doctor. But there were complications –the baby was breach—so the emergency hospital had to be called.

CHAPTER 3
GROWING UP
THE BEST I COULD

In 1936, we moved from 21st Street to Crocker Street, two blocks from the corner of 9th Place and San Pedro Street where Pop parked his truck to peddle fish. I was 7 years old, the age I began to notice a new world outside of my family.

On days when there was no school, Pop took me with him. I loved every bit of the trip, especially his morning stop when Pop would lift open the door to his large built-in icebox to display the fish inside. His scale was hung on a hook attached to his icebox. While other boys my age were playing at home, I was with my father amidst life in Chinatown on Alameda Street.

The traffic on Alameda Street was very busy. Big semi-trucks loaded with hay sped down the street like no one dared get in their way. I heard they were going to the stockyards farther South. The sidewalk shook as the heavy truck traffic rumbled by. Then the train came through on the way from the nearby train station to somewhere. I stood there watching as the loud noise came from the locomotives puffing and pulling the long line of passenger and freight cars. What fascinated me most was the screeching sound from the steel train wheels rubbing against the tracks. It was the most exciting moment for me. I saw all of this with my own eyes. Right there! By Pop's truck.

A customer came by and pointed to a fish he wanted. Pop used a short wooden pole with a nail protruding on the end to grab it. He made this tool by cutting a section of an old discarded broomstick. Then he weighed it and said in Chinese.

Fifty cents.

OK! The customer nodded.

I watched Pop scale the purchased fish, cut open its belly, pull out the guts, and dump them in a waste bucket, and then wash the fish in another bucket full of water. The customer paid him, and he placed the money in an abalone shell that he used as his cash register.

Another time, a cook from one of the restaurants came and motioned to Pop which fish he wanted for his kitchen. Then he left. Pop cleaned it, and I delivered the fish. When I got to the kitchen, the cook took the fish out of my bucket. Then I walked to the cashier's counter, waiting to be paid. He knew me and had no problem giving me the money. I was less than four feet tall, barely able to see over the counter. The cashier towered over me. I turned my face upwards to see his face. He looked like a giant staring down at me. Luckily, he had a smile. That helped a lot. It gave me some courage, and I felt less nervous standing there.

We lived downstairs, below the Low family. This home had three bedrooms. Uncle John had the front one. Mom, being a young inexperienced mother was learning how to properly raise children--- by trial and error. I was the second oldest. So, I received her mistakes as well as her successes. My older sister was the first and her darling. No problem taking care of her. The younger ones had it great. When it came to them, Mom knew what not to do--- I was the one she learned from. She felt I didn't need as much attention as the others. After all, I was the eldest son. It was time for me to have a bedroom by myself. The others had all the fun, sleeping together in the same room with Mom and Pop.

It was bedtime. Mom would be coming in to turn off the light. Then the dragon and ghost would come. Earlier, before bedtime, I climbed on a chair to reach the pull string for turning the ceiling light on or off. Then I tied a long string onto that pull string and tied the other end onto my bedpost by my pillow. Now if that dragon or ghost should appear, I could pull the string to turn on the light and scare them away as I lay frightened, with my head under my blanket.

Mom taught us the proper Cantonese etiquette. Every time I met Mr. Low, I greeted him:

Jo Sun! Low Boc.

Or in English, Good morning Uncle Low.

That was the proper greeting for a gentleman older than Pop. If he was younger than my father-- I would have said:

Low Sook.

Sook also meant uncle, but for a younger person. When I met some Chinese lady walking by, I was expected to say:

Moo.

or in English:

Madam.

Many times, I heard the greeting:

Sic Fan Mae?

For me, this was just another common polite greeting. I never questioned it. But back then, the older generation still carried traditions from their villages in China, from a time when famine was common. So, it was proper to say:

Have you eaten yet?

And the reply would be:

Yes, thank you, even though they may not have had enough to eat.

The Bakers lived next door. They were one of the few white families in the neighborhood. Jackie, their pet dog, always walked beside Mr. Baker. I don't remember seeing anyone walk their dogs on a leash. No one worried about vicious pets. They roamed freely on our street and always returned home when they felt like it.

I greeted him:

Hi, Mr. Baker!

I had a rich life growing up in a culture that was halfway between ancient China and modern-day America.

I often heard the phrase "*going back*," but I did not pay much attention to the saying. Later, I tried to make sense of this remark. *I was born here-- how could I be going back? To where?* It was the old folks yearning to return to the villages they had left behind.

I often wondered what direction life would have taken for me if Pop had not had the courage to quit his job washing dishes to become a fish peddler. He would have kept our apartment in old Chinatown and walked to work every day. Mom, my sister and I would have been very comfortable among our own kind, and life would have had few challenges. I am sure it cost him every dime he had to buy his used Ford panel truck, the fish from the wholesale commission sales store, and the ice he needed to keep the fish fresh.

He named his business "Joe Kee" and proudly painted the words in large capital words on the panels of both sides of his truck. Joe is the Cantonese pronunciation of his surname Chow. Joe Kee translates to "Chow's business." But others took it as his name, and he became known as Joe, although he was really named Harvey. Very few knew him by his correct name. Even Mom would all out:

Hey, Joe! Whenever she wanted to get his attention.

Our neighborhood on Crocker Street was Chinese, Mexicans, Japanese, and a few white folks. Pop's customers came from this area of two or three blocks. Most of the families depended on the economy the City Market created. That was where farmers trucked their crops to sell to the grocery stores and restaurants.

I remember hearing the adults talk about the "Red Russians." A neighborhood of White Russians lived not too far away, across from the Los Angeles River in Boyle Heights. The color designation had no relation to skin color. It defined a Russian as a Communist or non-Communist. One day, my uncle was having a conversation with a stranger. I heard a neighbor mention he was Red Russian. I kept staring at him. Why was his skin white, not red?

Another time, a group of we Chinese kids were sitting in our front yard. One of the children said we were the yellow race. So, we rolled up our sleeves, pulled up our shirts and looked at each other's skin. We couldn't find any yellow. We only knew yellow as the color of a crayon. These were the innocent days. We were 7 years old, trying to make sense of this confusing world.

Elementary school was no help. One teacher was Chinese. The others were Caucasians. They didn't understand us.

Can you tell me when you have your salads? Before the meal or after? Miss Taylor, my sixth-grade teacher asked.

What is she talking about? Our main dish was set in the middle of the table, and each of us had a bowl of rice, and we picked up the meat or vegetables with our chopsticks.

What is a salad? I wondered

I sat quietly, saying nothing as she continued as if we all understood her. Then she continued:

Do not eat only starches. Eat some greens.

Starch? Our basic food was rice, not potatoes nor bread. We had sandwiches for lunch, but never ate bread with our main meal.

Another time, she told the class the best part of a vegetable are the green leaves, not the white stems. I always liked the white stems. It was just me. The rest of the family would agree with her. They would rather eat only the greens. Mom always said:

Never contradict a teacher. You are just a student. Show your respect.

I wanted to say: *I like the white stems better than the green ones.*

But what Mom said about how a student should behave towards a teacher held me back. It was better to keep quiet.

She also told us how to look at the traffic signal before crossing the street:

Children, you do not cross until the signal is green.

That's not what Mom told us! We children shouted.

Mom said cross only when the signal is red.

She kept insisting. We kept shouting.

No! Mom is right----you cross only on the red light.

Looking back, I can imagine her misunderstanding. She was accustomed to traveling by car and was telling us how to cross the street as if we were in a car. We were from poorer areas, and we walked most of the time. The street crossings we made were in front of the cars.

The teachers came from a different culture. I pictured life differently, but eventually I began to understand what they tried to teach us, and that gradually redirected me toward the mainstream culture.

CHAPTER 4
MY PRE-ADOLESCENT
LIFE EXPERIENCES

One semester, I believe it was in 1938, a new group of Chinese children appeared at 9th Street School. They did not speak English and had Chinese names spelled in English. The names were Him Li, Chu Wong, Wah Yee, etc.

Can you speak Chinese? the teacher asked me.

Yes, I can, I replied.

Take Him Li outside and help him read this book in English. she directed.

They were from the families that went to Hong Kong during the Great Depression, then came back to escape the advancing Japanese soldiers. Somehow, I felt different from them. They didn't act like my friends or me and were more comfortable with others from Hong Kong. Yet, we were all ethnically Chinese. I think the difference was in the way we thought. Our thoughts were in English, while theirs were in Chinese. Eventually, we became accustomed to each other and our differences slowly disappeared.

Another influence I had was from my Chinese language school. What a big difference compared to 9th Street School! Our parents respected the schoolmaster highly. He was the kind of teacher our parents wanted, a no-nonsense strict disciplinarian.

The parents of the students grew up in the old tradition where the teacher was a respected scholar. *"He is right, and you listen."* But for us, he was a relic of ancient times that could not be questioned by the students.

Chinese writing does not use the alphabet. There are some key parts of the characters that help a person pronounce the words, but still, it requires memory to become literate. I did not have memory skills. I tried drawing simple pictures next to the words, hoping they would help. They didn't. Then I used the alphabet to write the sounds next to each character. That helped a little. Anyway, I did not meet the teacher's expectation. I could not read Chinese as well as the others in my class.

I spent hours studying my Chinese lessons, and whenever I faced this teacher, his stern demeanor scared the daylights out of me. All the hours I had spent studying disappeared the instant I looked into his eyes. He thought I never tried to study. He didn't know how many times I tried. He just didn't know how to teach! He was educated in Chinese literature and history, but had no training for teaching.

Lessons were held in a rented house that was converted into classrooms. The operating expense was funded by the tuition paid by our parents. Classes started at 4:30 p.m. and ended at 6:30 p.m. Monday through Friday. Saturday class was half day from 9:00 am to noon. The curriculum was reading and writing in Chinese and the history of China during the decline of the Ching Dynasty. Although I did not like his teaching methods---his lessons gave me a valuable appreciation of my cultural heritage.

On the Ninth Street elementary school playground during recess, a different problem confronted me. I had no athletic ability. The boys never wanted me on their team. Whenever I had the opportunity to join them, nothing went right. I couldn't hang onto the baseball bat like the others. The baseball bat flew into the air as I missed the ball.

The boys wouldn't let me play any position except right field. That is where I could do the least damage to their game. Batters usually hit the ball to left field, not right field. Once in a while, a ball flew towards right field. I stood there, eyes glued on it as it came towards me, ready to catch the ball. I said to myself,

Got to catch the ball, everybody is watching me, hope this time I do it right.

The ball went right through my hands and fell onto the ground by my foot. I stood in right field embarrassed. I felt useless. The boys on my team hated what happened. They didn't want me on their team. But they had no choice, because the teacher insisted on my participation.

Several other boys were also not as physically mature. But I was the smallest and the least among them, the bottom of the social playground.

George was a playground outcast like me. He had a different take on life. Although his family was poor, somehow his childhood was different. His parents were among the Okies that came to California after losing every penny they had, just like my parents had lost everything in the Sacramento Delta. There was a huge difference between us. He was white and had an unlimited future ahead of him. I was constantly reminded of my low place in society.

George believed everyone should have an equal opportunity to play. So, he approached the teacher and asked permission to form a team of those left out. Again, they would not choose me on their team. I was the least physically fit. Despite being left out, I admired his attitude.

He and I were in the same graduating class from elementary school. We went to Lafayette Junior High, a predominately Black school. George impressed me as being a very decent person. He had no hesitation making friends among the Black kids and played with them with no feelings of being different.

John was another boy that I remember. He was Black and came from another school district nearby. I remember hearing the teacher tell him he had to return to the 20th Street school.

There was something different about him. He was not aggressive, but polite. I noticed this and somehow never forgot him. He had a greatness that shone above the other boys. He must have come from a good home with intelligent parents. Many years later, I learned he not only became an organist at his church, but also a high school principal.

A6 was the last class before junior high.

The sixth graders wore a blue and yellow ribbon tied together in a bow with two short streamers dangling down. The girls wore theirs on their blouses near their shoulders, and the boys wore theirs near their belts on their trousers. They were the elite.

I noticed Oscar, one of the sixth graders. He had started to grow his hair long and combed toward the back of his head, like a ducktail.

I asked him,

Why don't you get a haircut?

*I am growing a pachuco, h*e answered.

He wanted to be like most of the older boys in junior high. They wore their trousers baggy, and the bottom cuff was small, just barely wide enough to put a foot though. They were the zoot suiters, much like the hippies that came later, with the same in-your-face attitude. It was their show of independence—their lives were as important as the established, more "genteel" crowd.

I met Robert at La Fayette Jr. High. We played together. Robert was Mexican, and Jarvis was white Oakie.

What is your last name? I asked Robert when we met.

Brown, he replied.

That isn't Mexican, I remarked.

My father is American, and my mother is Mexican, he explained.

You are lucky. With that name, you will have more opportunities, I commented.

I had heard stories from adults about discrimination and knew that was the life ahead of me.

What are you talking about? Jarvis asked.

I looked at Robert, and he nodded. He understood. Both Robert and I said no more, and the three of us continued as friends.

Jarvis and I were good friends. One day, he wanted me to go with him to Biminis Beach. It was a private indoor pool located on the west side. Children paid to swim there. Just as we approached the entrance to buy a ticket, another young boy whispered to Jarvis.

They are not going to let him in.

He motioned at me. Jarvis couldn't understand.

Come on, they can't do that, Jarvis said to me.

But I understood and did not want that person in the ticket booth to say something unpleasant to me. So, I said:

Let's do something else, I quietly said to Jarvis.

We went to West Lake Park, rented a small boat on the lake and had fun together.

Of all the many experiences I had growing up, one in particular had the greatest influence on me. The WPA (Work Program Administration) was constructing a storm drain along Crocker Street. As I watched the workmen digging the trench and installing huge concrete pipes, Uncle John asked me,

What do you want to be when you grow up?

I was around 8 years old and admired the worker pushing the wheelbarrow. That was what I wanted to do. So, I pointed to the worker.

I want to be like him.

Oh! So, you want to be an engineer. Uncle John faced me and spoke.

I didn't know what an engineer was and thought he meant the laborer that pushed the wheelbarrow. But that thought stuck with me.

Our neighborhood friends
Crocker Street, Los Angeles Calif.
1937

Birthday Party for Brother Ted at our Home on Crocker St.
Teddy is the smallest of the group.
Lower photo: Teddy on his birthday present.
1937

CHAPTER 5
OTTO ZIMMERMAN

There were five of us. My sister, me, and three other kids from our street. We were on our way home from a trip to Griffith Park, all riding in Otto Zimmerman's blue Willy sedan. It was such a wonderful time. How I remember those days. Otto Zimmerman made that possible. He took us see the La Brea Tar Pits, hike in the hills of Griffith Park, spend a day going to Calico, places we hadn't known. I do not remember how he came into our lives. But it happened one day;

Otto appeared on our street
Like an Angel sent from heaven
Driven by love for humanity
With only one purpose in mind
Bring the children to God

He was a total stranger that one day came to our home --- knocked on the door and spoke to Mom.

May I take your children to Sunday School? It is at the First Free Methodist Church on Sixth Street.

Otto became part of our community, not only with the children, but also with many of the older Chinese. This was around 1937, when I was eight years old.

For some unknown reason, Mom trusted him. She let him take us to Sunday School. He was a young bachelor. During the week, his occupation was "handy man." His customers were from the white community, not ours.

I remember Sunday School started with the lay minister leading the singing and speaking to the congregation. Everyone sat together in the main sanctuary. We were Otto's children, and he sat with us. The congregation was all white folks still living in the neighborhood and others who had moved away but returned every Sunday to support the church.

Then everyone sang. "We are marching to Zion, beautiful, beautiful Zion, the city of God" as we walked to our class.

The boys' class was in the balcony overlooking the main sanctuary. Otto was our Sunday School teacher. The first thing he would do was pass a small cardboard bank around, and we would give a penny to the church. Then he began his lesson. He did not read the Bible to us, but instead explained how we should behave so that God would be pleased with us.

It is wrong to say bad words like "God damn." Why would you ask God to damn someone?

Another time, he talked about discrimination. He said it was wrong, and people should not be that way. Although we were just eight or ten years old, we were well aware of this attitude toward us. We encountered this kind of treatment whenever we left our neighborhood. But Otto expressed himself in such a way that we did not develop any bad feelings toward anyone.

The most enjoyable time we had was during a school holiday when he took us to the abandoned mines in Calico. Otto made sandwiches and brought a quart of milk for lunch. When we got to Calico, he stopped the car, and we got outside and sat on the boulders scattered along the dirt road. Then he handed a paper bag to us and said,

Take one sandwich and pass the bag around.

Then he handed the bottle of milk to me and said,

Take a sip and pass it on.

We were bewildered. Our parents had taught us to never drink nor eat from the same cups or dishes or utensils someone else used. It was not sanitary.

So, after I took a drink, no one else was willing to drink from the same bottle.

Otto noticed and said nothing, but the next time, he brought paper cups. He handed the bottle of milk to my friend and passed paper cups to each of us.

Don't throw away the cups when you finish drinking. I will take them home and wash them, so we can use them again.

He had grown as a young man on his own and had learned to survive frugally. He didn't think that was anything unusual. After all, those were hard times.

I have been using these cups for about three years, he said.

Yipes! These paper cups? my older sister exclaimed.

After lunch, he let us explore the abandoned tunnels by ourselves. It was fun.

That is something no adult would allow today. We could have fallen into some of the pits and gotten injured. But that was 1937. Life was much more innocent, and our parents never thought of the many things we fear today.

He loved the desert around Barstow, and on many weekends, he would take us there to enjoy ourselves. On the way home from one trip, we ran into a thick layer of fog as he drove over the mountain highway.

We couldn't see anything in front of us. Otto slowed down and drove very carefully. We thought it was the most exciting part of the trip and enjoyed every bit of it.

One summer, Otto got Mom's permission to take us to the Free Methodist Church retreat at Thousand Pines near Lake Arrowhead. I faintly remember going there in the church bus. It was a first experience for me. We had Bible classes, and most of the time, we enjoyed the forest of pine trees. There were also craft making classes.

While we were there, a small fire broke out in the forest. It was quickly put out, and we were told something about it. I can't remember much about what was said, but we were alerted to that danger.

My friend and I walked into the forest shouting "Timber," pretending we were cutting down trees. As we were play-acting, a young lady camp counselor appeared.

Why are you playing with matches? She asked in a demeaning voice.

We aren't playing with matches, I replied.

Some children saw you lighting a fire. She accused us in a scolding manner.

That is a lie. We didn't do that. I shouted.

Hand over your matches to me, she demanded.

We don't have any. Check our pockets! I pleaded.

She said nothing, just stared at us and walked away. I saw that familiar look on her face, the look of disdain. It made me feel unwanted. Fortunately, Otto had talked to us about discrimination and told us not to harbor bad feelings against another person. It was his way of leading us to God.

Many years later, Otto married and lived in Barstow for the remainder of his life. During those years, he kept in touch with our community, and we were lifelong friends. Otto kept in contact with me, even up to the time I was married and had a family. He came to visit me while I lived in West Los Angeles in the Sawtelle area. Although he moved away, I still heard from him via his postcards.

CHAPTER 6

THE YEARS 1936 THROUGH 1940

I stood by Mom's bedroom door and watched her take a butter knife and poke it into the slot on top of her piggy bank. She was in tears as she desperately emptied out every coin. I felt her sadness but couldn't understand what was going on. How could I? I was too young to realize how hard Pop worked to earn enough to not only feed us, but also pay the rent. The Depression hit us very hard. If Pop couldn't pay the rent, we could be evicted and have to move again. Peddling fish, Pop barely made enough to support us. I was nine years old. The year was 1938.

We had just moved across the street from a three-bedroom unit of a duplex to a single- family home with a large garage. Entry to the garage was from the alley, and this gave us some privacy. Pop struggled to build his fish business; he would approach the cooks at the Chinese restaurants offering to sell them shrimp, already peeled. This eliminated their need for extra help in the kitchen, so they bought them. I spent hours sitting in the garage with Mom peeling the shells off shrimp.

It took all of us working as a family to back up Pop's business—to survive financially. I never gave any thought to how crowded we lived. As long as I can remember, Uncle Joe lived with us. Every time Uncle John was between jobs, he also lived with us. We were just one happy family.

I can still picture our home. It had two bedrooms, a kitchen, a dining room, and a living room. By then, there were five children in our family. I had two sisters, Prudy and Pat, and two brothers, Stanley and Ted. Every room except the kitchen was used to sleep in. I shared the dining room with Uncle Joe, and Uncle John slept in the living room. He had to share the living room space with all of us each evening because this was where the radio was. After dinner, everyone sat around the radio listening to the Hit Parade, Red Skelton, and other popular programs. My favorite was Luigi. It always started out with Luigi writing a letter back to his mother in Italy, with *"Dear Mama Mia."* Then there was Shultz, a jovial German immigrant with his foreign accent. He was in adult evening class learning to be American. I could identify with the plot because it reminded me of our life.

I didn't know we were poor, but my parents felt it. Many families were suffering the same way. Mom always worried each time rent was due. But somehow, we managed, and the rent was paid on time. I knew several families whose fathers worked, but often were not fully employed. I played with those children, and they felt we were rich because we always had fish for supper. Having fish was a luxury. Pop cooked whatever fish he could not sell. Our friends did not have such an advantage. Some of my friends had to go to the City Market and salvage the rejected vegetables from the disposal bins for their meals. These were not spoiled but were not good enough for the buyers at the City Market.

I became aware of these hard times only because Mom told us what was happening. There were several names etched in my mind. Many times, Mom told us how they helped Pop. To this day, I can still remember their good deeds. Each bit of kindness may have seemed like a normal pursuit of business to some other person. But as Mom told us, it meant they wanted Pop to succeed. Pop's opportunities came because people lent him a helping hand and opened doors for him.

I recall Mom telling us about a seafood salesman. His name sounded like Tankich. One day, he approached Pop.

Joe! I want to put aside 1,000 pounds of shrimp for you, he offered.

He was the regional sales person for a wholesale shrimp company in Southern California.

But I do not have the money for that much shrimp, Pop said.

Don't worry, I will set aside 1,000 pounds for you, and you take whatever you can afford and pay for it, Tankich responded.

This was a huge break for Pop. Now he had a guaranteed supply of shrimp and he could go to the Chinese restaurants and ask if he could supply them.

Pop met another wonderful person, Michael. He raised frogs and also fished in Lake Elsinore. He wanted to supply Pop with live frogs and live carps. That was just what the Chinese wanted. So, Pop had a large tank about six feet long, four feet wide and three feet deep built and placed in our back yard. He kept the fish alive for days and was able to have fresh carp to sell every day.

Those men were just two of those who came into our lives and opened doors of opportunity for Pop; he could not have gotten by without their help.

I grew up witnessing the struggle my parents had, starting from rock bottom to becoming financially comfortable. I saw the hardship and learned from my parents to keep fighting and not give up. I also saw that my parents could not have reached their success without some help.

One day, a man asked Pop if he would be interested in buying the poultry business that was on the corner where he sold fish. He owned the building and hired a manager to run the business. They kept live chickens in coops, and as a chicken was sold, it was taken to the back room where it was slaughtered, cleaned, and dressed. Business was poor and losing money, but Pop was interested. That evening, he told Mom and asked for her opinion. Mom was excited and told him to take the gamble, and said she would work with him to build the business.

They had some savings in the bank and divided the store into two separate businesses. One side sold fresh fish, and the other side sold poultry. Pop managed the fish side and Mom, the poultry side. Somehow, Pop was able to work both sides to do the heavy work. Mom handled the money.

Mom told me there were days when not one chicken was sold. Luckily, Pop had a steady business selling fish. She also told us that when the store was completely separated into two sections, all they had left in their pocket was $9. But they had a large walk-in refrigerator, a very nice showcase to display fish, and a private office to conduct business.

Whenever possible, I had to be at the store helping clean fish or chicken for the customers. Other children enjoyed themselves playing, but I was thrust into the adult world.

CHAPTER 7
FAMILY TIME AT
THE DINNER TABLE

It was November, the beginning of three big holidays, Thanksgiving, Christmas and New Year. The weather was still great, no rain. I played on the street with my friends while Mom prepared the Thanksgiving meal. Then around 4 pm, the turkey was cooked and the table set. Everyone, Uncle Joe, Uncle John, Mom and Pop and we children, sat down. We were having a homemade banquet. We could feel the eagerness from everyone ready to eat this special feast of turkey, yams, mashed potatoes and bread stuffing with gravy. Yummy. This was happy family time. Everyone was having a great time talking and eating. We were almost finished eating when someone asked:

Where's Teddy?

No one had noticed he was still out front, playing with neighbor kids.

What? No one had missed him?

Uncle John rushed to the front door and shouted.

Teddy, come in now! Everybody is almost finished eating.

Teddy was 8 years old, my little brother. He was having too much fun playing with his friends and did not hear Mom calling us in for dinner. "Dinner at 4 o'clock?" We usually ate at 6 o'clock pm. But today was Thanksgiving, not just an ordinary everyday meal. But to Teddy, this was when mothers were busy cooking, and all the children were having great fun playing out on the street.

He was the youngest and fast! I watched him run down the street toward us, just as eager for the Thanksgiving dinner as the rest of us. Luckily, he couldn't eat as much as us. There was still plenty of food for him.

Almost every month, there was a special meal day. We celebrated all the traditional American holidays, and the Chinese ones that Pop knew were observed in China. Times had improved. World War II ended the Depression. Having a good meal was no longer a dream.

Mom had prepared the Thanksgiving, Easter, Christmas and New Year dinners, plus the birthday parties, and Pop cooked for the traditional Chinese feasts to celebrate the passing of winter, Chinese New Year and other holidays. Why? Because Pop was the only one knowledgeable about them. We just enjoyed the feasts he cooked.

There is one Chinese specialty food that Mom cooked. The Cantonese called it Joong. Making Joong was a family project. We sat around the table as Mom told us how to first fold the bamboo leaves, fill them half full with sweet rice, add a slice of ham, a piece of barbecued pork, white beans, and the egg yolk of a salted duck egg, and a thick slice of bacon, finish with more sweet rice, then fold the leaves to wrap in an angular shape and tie together with a string. It took hours of boiling in water until the sweet rice was sticky. One of them was a small meal. It was my favorite and cooked for a special day celebrating a legend of ancient Chinese folklore. Today, it can be purchased any time at Chinese restaurants or grocery stores.

Pop cooked meals that not only celebrated special days, but they were also beneficial to our health. When summer began to change to fall, he always made a soup of watercress boiled with a chunk of pork liver and cooked for hours until the entire flavor was in the soup. He believed that the nutrients from the watercress and liver helped build immunity against sickness before winter. He emphasized to us that our bodies needed to adjust to a change in weather, and the nutrients in his soup nourished our resistance to sickness.

Sometimes, Pop decided to cook won ton. I enjoyed that time together with Mom and my brothers and sisters. Pop would prepare the ground pork, mixed together with ground shrimp, shitake mushrooms and green onions. He added the spices, then cracked open an egg and mixed it with the pork. Pop placed a bowl of the prepared meat mixture in the middle of the table. This was the time that gave me the feeling we were family. Everyone sat with a butter knife in hand, ready to wrap a dab of the meat mixture as Mom supervised us. I followed her instructions and wrapped the won ton in the flour skin, ready for Pop to cook it in boiling water. In the meantime, Pop cooked a special vegetable soup to be eaten with the won ton. I felt so happy and excited, enjoying a family feast that all of us helped prepare.

Another time, it was chow mien. This time, only Pop did the work. Then another time, Pop took a winter melon gourd, scraped out the seeds and kept the top, just like with a pumpkin on Halloween. Then he added pieces of fresh duck, lotus seeds, bamboo shoots, mushrooms, some salt and pepper into the hollowed-out melon. He placed the top of the melon back on and steamed it for several hours. Pop placed the cooked melon on a large dish in the middle of the table and scooped out a portion into an empty rice bowl for each one of us. We ate it as the main meal. The other vegetables and meats were just fillers. Those are the days I remember. No other event could be happier than family time at the dinner table.

CHAPTER 8
GROWING UP ON SAN PEDRO STREET

P op handed me the bucket of fish he had just cleaned.

Take this to Modern Café, he said to me.

I gladly did what he told me. I knew the rewards that were coming. I walked through the café past all the patrons sitting at the counter eating. They knew who I was. I entered the kitchen and handed the bucket of fish to the cook. He dumped it into his sink, and before giving me back the bucket, took a fresh baked bun, brushed melted butter on it, cut a slice of roast pork, placed it in the bun and handed it to me. What a treat! It was delicious.

Business at the City Market began to wind down about 9:00 am. The wholesale commission houses sold the produce the farmers brought in, and the trucks were loaded to make the deliveries. Crowds of farmers, laborers, and merchants were walking up and down the one block of San Pedro Street from 9th Place to 10th Street. Everyone seemed to know each other. It was a friendly gathering of like-minded people. They were shopping for dinner. Their day was done, and they were ready to go home. But for Pop and the local merchants, the work day had just begun.

Zankich, a fisherman from Terminal Island in the Los Angeles Harbor, arrived at our store. He had called earlier and told Pop what he had caught, white sea bass and sculpin, just what Pop's customers liked. He made his order.

I take one box of sea bass and one box of sculpin.

A fish box is about 18 inches wide by four feet long and twelve inches deep. That holds a lot of fish. He arrived in his pickup truck, and they greeted each other like old friends. Then Pop and Zankich, each using a gaffing hook, grabbed each end of the box and loaded it onto Pop's steel cart. Some of the fish were still alive. Those were the days when "fresh" meant just caught. The customers saw them unloading the fish, and soon a small crowd gathered and began choosing what they wanted, before Pop even had a chance to push the cart into the store. Then he took out what they wanted, cleaned it and wrapped it in butcher paper. Pop had no time to place the fish in his showcase. It could wait til this rush was over.

For me, this was just an ordinary no school day. Other children were playing at home, but I was helping at the store. I grew up amongst workers and business people, while at the same time, enjoying childhood games with friends. San Pedro Street was the dividing line between the commercial area and our neighborhood of families. The large semi-trailer trucks, the drivers and the produce they brought to the City Market were as familiar to me and my friends as flying a kite or playing with marbles.

One incident happened when I was about twelve years old. Everyone was talking about a new parking enforcement policeman. He rode his three-wheel motorcycle and marked the tires of parked vehicles, so he could see which ones had exceeded their time limit. He took advantage of his authority to garner free vegetables or other favors in return for allowing minor parking violations. This allowed more time for customers to shop. However, he was greedy, demanded a lot, and was disliked. One day, I noticed he had disappeared.

Where is the motorcycle policeman? I asked.

Oh, there was an accident, someone said.

What accident? I asked.

Well one day, while he was driving by on his motorcycle marking tire, a whole stack of crated vegetables accidentally fell off a truck and sent him to the hospital.

Somehow, from then on, there was no more harassing the truckers.

I remember Charlie Kincaid. He was a Black man living alone in an apartment on Olympic Blvd. and San Pedro Street. I am not sure how old he was, probably a few years older than Pop. Charlie was just one of those who would often come to our store just to say hello. Our store was some place where he felt at home. One day, Pop wanted to go for a cup of coffee and asked him to look after the store. Business was slow, and Pop was alone.

Pop just thought of Charlie as just another person in our neighborhood. But to Charlie, this meant a lot; someone gave no thought to him being Black and trusted him. One day, Charlie told my sister and me:

I like your father. I watch your store. No one steals from your father.

At that moment, as he spoke, even though both my sister and I were very young, we had this feeling in our hearts. It is hard to explain. Perhaps, it was a sense of pride for my father because he saw Charlie as just another person he trusted. Pop was fair-minded and did not unfairly prejudge Charlie because he was Black.

It has been forty years since I left the neighborhood. One day, I went back to visit San Pedro Street in Los Angeles. I leaned against the familiar lamppost in front of the store building and began dreaming. The abandoned corner building where Pop's store stood shuttered, lifeless, and vacant, seemed to suddenly come to life. Everything came back in a ghostly manner. Mom was sitting on a chair chatting with a friend. I could hear the conversation, but the ghostly figures could not see nor hear me. Minnie, my old Cocker Spaniel, was there lying next to the baby carriage with my sister Pam in it. Minnie wouldn't let anyone come close to Pam. There was a metal tub full of live frogs and a screen cover on top to keep them in. Then this white man, Raymond, came by. My parents knew him. He often came for a friendly chat. I remember that conversation.

Hey Joe! Where did you get these frogs? Raymond asked.

Oh! Somebody laised them, Pop answered.

Everyone broke out in laughter, but Pop stood there, puzzled. He gave an honest answer; he did not realize he could not pronounce the "R" in raise correctly. It sounded like he said someone laid them.

The memories kept appearing. I saw Pop surrounded by Mexican women. His excuse—

I am learning Spanish.

He is not fooling me, Mom told me.

I know he is enjoying the company and attention from all those pretty young Mexican ladies.

Those were the old days, when business in the late afternoon was usually slow. The store was a gathering place for socializing. Many older Chinese men would come in, and Pop would leave the Chinese language newspaper out for them to read. It was a good friendly atmosphere.

As I stood on that corner looking down the block, it was again ten in the morning. The City Market had completed business. Then a voice spoke up.

Hey Joe! I want a big fat pullet. Can you have it ready for me by noon?

All light, I go dress one light away, I heard Pop reply.

I see Pop instructing the worker to pick out a good fat chicken from a cage, slaughter it, and have it cleaned and wrapped, ready for pick up in an hour, as he continues to place his fish in his iced-up show case. This is his peak business time. All the produce delivery trucks at the City Market are loaded and ready to leave. The crates of vegetables are designated for delivery to the retail grocery stores and restaurants.

The market men and the farmers that trucked in their vegetables are through for the day that started at 3 am. Now they begin to buy the groceries for tonight's meal, and Pop's day has begun. The cafe's---Modern Cafe', New York Cafe', and Tai Loy Cafe'---have come to life, filled with men from the City Market.

It felt good daydreaming about those happy days. Then I woke to reality; the businesses are boarded up, vacant and lifeless, waiting to die. The grocery store, restaurants, and cafe's are just memories. None exist today.

Back in those days, homeless men lived together on a vacant lot on Olympic Boulevard by the alley between San Pedro Street and Crocker. They were the hobos broken in spirit. I often talked with them, and one of them told me his wife had died, and he had no money. Then he began to cry.

Why do you have to cry? asked the man next to him.

I can't help it. he replied, sobbing.

I just stood there. I was only twelve years old, but somehow, I understood.

Our store was a stopping place for familiar faces who just enjoyed socializing. Both Mom and Pop were always willing to spend time chatting with people. It was a friendly atmosphere where everyone was relaxed and happy.

The men who came to America during those early days were mostly bachelors. They were sojourners hoping to earn enough and return to China to live a good, comfortable life there. Many of them lived together, and gambling was their recreation.

Some of the businesses on San Pedro Street were fronts for illegal gambling. There was a tacit understanding with the law enforcement, and that way of life continued quietly. I remember one store selling magazines. They probably did not comply with the unwritten rule; they had strung an electrical conduit over the roof with a hidden buzzer by the corner of the building. A lookout stood by this buzzer every day to warn gamblers of approaching plainclothes detectives. But somehow, the authorities knew and outsmarted them in a surprise raid.

I remember seeing men running. The slower ones got caught and were sent to jail. I remember the noise. Bang! Bang! Bang! It was the sound of sledge hammers tearing apart the gambling tables. Later that afternoon, the carpenters came to make repairs. Someone said there was a new precinct officer in charge, and he was letting them know. Need I say more?

CHAPTER 9
MY GODFATHER

I shouted:

Hi, Mr. Jang!

Then he would come over to me, laughing at everything I said. Mom said:

You should speak to him with more courtesy. Not like one child to another. Show a little more respect to an older person.

She reminded me that I was only thirteen years old. He didn't mind. He loved every bit of it. I am not sure how he became my godfather. I felt closer to him than to Pop because he spoke English fluently, and Pop always spoke Cantonese to us. I couldn't express myself well enough in Chinese.

Pop's fish and poultry store occupied the corner unit of his four-unit commercial building. He and his partner supplied the Chinese restaurants and local Chinese grocery stores with the noodles they made. Back in the 1940's, there were only two Chinese noodle factories in Los Angeles. He named his "The Hong Kong Noodle Factory." They made the noodles from the dough they had prepared the night before. His partner then made the deliveries, and that is when he came by our store to visit.

Godfather and his partner also had a 60-acre farm in Artesia on the southwest corner of Norwalk and Del Amo. Lee, a man about my father's age, lived on the farm and managed it. The crop was asparagus on thirty acres and leafy vegetables on the other thirty acres. Every Sunday, before he drove to Artesia to see how the crops were growing and find out if Lee had any needs, he stopped by my house to take me with him.

The only world I knew was my neighborhood and the children I played with. I heard the boys in school talking about the fun they had vacationing at places the All Nations Club took them. All Nations was something like the YMCA. The organization was located a mile away from where I lived. But I knew nothing about the advantages they wanted to give us.

My good time, something the other children did not have, was riding in the truck with Godfather, going out to the country, away from the city, and enjoying the wide-open space, especially smelling the fresh country air.

As soon as we left the city, he would tell me to sit on the driver's seat, and he would teach me how to drive. You can imagine how a thirteen- year old boy drove. Mom told me:

You really scared him when you drove too fast. Especially when you drove over the narrow lane across the bridge.

I thought the air out in the countryside was special. It never dawned on me that I had become accustomed to the odor from all the chicken droppings in the cages in our poultry shop. Many times, some women would pinch their noses while ordering a chicken from us. I thought they were snobbish. I didn't realize how badly the store smelled.

When we got to the farm, Godfather went with Lee to look over the crops. He left me alone to enjoy looking for horn toads, going into the barn to see the chickens and handing hay to the horse. You have no idea how refreshing that day was to me.

On the way home from the farm, my special time was when he stopped in the town of Artesia. We sat on the sandwich counter to have a milkshake. He let me choose the flavor. Most of the time, I chose vanilla, sometimes strawberry. Then he would order the same for himself. Those were the days when the drinks were thick with good ice cream and milk poured from a bottle. I can still picture myself sitting inside the drug store, ten cents for a milkshake and fifteen cents for malt.

When we arrived back from the farm, he would drop me off at my home. After supper, he returned and took me to the movies.

I loved listening to his stories. He told me he wanted a social life, and so he decided to attend the Presbyterian Church located on Adams Street just west of San Pedro Street. He had never been to Sunday services and was not sure how to dress. So, he did the best he could. He went to a tuxedo rental store and got a formal outfit. It had a tail like he had seen in some pictures.

That Sunday morning, he walked along the front entryway and noticed that everyone else was dressed casually. No one wore formal wear. He was ridiculously overdressed. It was too late to change. He hurriedly loosened his waist belt, stuffed the coat tails into his trousers, hoping no one would notice. The boys saw him and teased him by pulling the tails out of his pants, laughing at him. Godfather was laughing as he told me how embarrassed he was. Then he said the boy that harassed him the most became his partner in business ventures., as well as becoming his brother-in-law.

Another story I enjoyed hearing was how he and his friends spent the day after church service. They brought along their .22 caliber rifles, and then placed them in the cloak closet til after church service. Then they took their .22 rifles, boarded the streetcar on San Pedro Street, transferred to another streetcar on Broadway, and when they got to the outskirts of town and open fields, shot at rabbits from the street car window. He recalled when the City of Los Angeles had passed a law prohibiting spittoons on the streetcars. He said:

Everyone was mad. Where can they spit when chewing tobacco?

He talked to me like someone who understood me. When he told me his stories, I felt like we belonged with each other. To this day, the memories I have of spending Sundays with him is a childhood experience I shall never forget.

One Sunday, as he drove along Pioneer Blvd. just before turning left onto Del Amo, a chicken ran in front of us and got killed. It happened suddenly, without warning. Godfather quickly stopped the truck and picked up the chicken. At that moment, I expected him to toss it onto the side of the road. To my surprise, he tossed it onto the truck, and when we got to the farm, we had fried chicken for lunch.

When I reached 15 years old, I began to spend more time with my neighborhood friends and less time with Godfather. I did not want to intrude into his family and slowly drifted away from him. I could have made him very happy, but I did not want to dominate his feelings, as I felt I should with my father. Although I remained close to him, he rightfully belonged to his two daughters.

CHAPTER 10
WORLD WAR II

My Sister Prudy and my brother Stanley and I were returning from a movie downtown on Broadway. Just as we got to Ninth Place, our street, we noticed everyone was excitedly talking. Japan had attacked and bombed Pearl Harbor. Our Japanese neighbors were stunned. They didn't know what to expect. On Monday, the next day, all the Japanese children were absent from school.

The following week, I noticed plainclothes policemen in front of the Japanese businesses on San Pedro Street. Young men on our street went to sign up for the military, but there was a problem. Most people couldn't tell the Chinese from the Japanese. So, our elders had buttons made that said "*Chinese American.*" We pinned them on our clothes.

World War II had begun. A Japanese family on 9th Place was one of the many ordered to leave for a relocation camp. Their house was a half block from our store and very convenient for my parents. Pop immediately rented it, and we moved in. Now we had the luxury of a two-story home with three bedrooms. What a big improvement in living standards! Besides that, we were just a short walk to the store. Our Cocker Spaniel Minnie freely went from the house to the store whenever she chose. Nothing could be better. There was very little change in our neighborhood after the Japanese left. Life continued uninterrupted. I was too young to have any opinion about the situation or to wonder what happened to that family.

Uncle Joe had been married for three years and had two daughters. He volunteered for the Army Air Force and became a fighter pilot flying P40 Warhawks and P-47 Thunderbolts. He flew antisubmarine patrol from Iceland and later flew as fighter escort for the bombers on raids over Europe. Uncle John wanted to sign up for the Army, but the recruiter told him he was above draft age and didn't need to sign up. Besides, he was born in China. Uncle John insisted, saying this was his home and he wanted to fight for America. I do not remember exactly what happened, but I think within two weeks of joining the Army, a newspaper in San Diego had an article about Uncle John receiving full citizenship from the judge.

Uncle John was in the Quartermasters in the Army. He experienced the return to the Philippines and the invasion of the Mariana Islands. He told my sister about one of his landings on a South Pacific Island occupied by Japanese soldiers. When the gate on the landing craft came down, everyone rushed ashore to secure a beachhead. Uncle John was too short and would have drowned in the deep water. His buddy grabbed onto him until they reached shallow water. He was not from Texas, but Uncle John referred to him as Tex. They were very close friends.

Uncle John was running behind Tex as they ran toward onto the beach. Then Tex got shot and died in front of him. Although this had happened years ago, Uncle John could not keep his tears from rolling down his face as he said:

Tex got the bullet and I lived.

Many things happened in the month after the bombing of Pearl Harbor. I remember the labor unions wanted a pay raise and called a strike to make their demands. It was all over the newspapers. Then the next day, they formed a picket line in front of the entrance of the aircraft manufacturing plants. I recall seeing photos of Army men with loaded fifty caliber machine guns pointing them at the men picketing, warning them not to obstruct the entrance to the aircraft plant. The strike ended immediately.

Food rationing started, and cigarettes were scarce. Lines of people stood waiting to buy cigarettes whenever they became available. I did not want to be like them. So, I never wanted to start smoking cigarettes.

The war plants were humming 24 hours a day. I heard some people held two jobs by working two different shifts in 24 hours. Restaurants were busy with lines of would-be diners waiting to get in. The same went for theaters.

Our physical education teacher became a streetcar driver early in the morning before class began at La Fayette Junior High. His streetcar route passed by the school, and each morning as he drove by while we were walking to school, he would slow down and kept ringing the streetcar bell.

Ding, ding, ding!

He waved his hand, hailing us to get on for a free ride to La Fayette.

Opportunity came suddenly. Who would have guessed that when Pop and Mom bought the poultry business back in 1939 that a war would begin and usher in prosperity for us? Every morning before Pop opened the door to sell, there was a line of customers waiting to buy. There were so many at the store that we just slaughtered chickens as fast our workers could manage. No one cared how large or how small each chicken was; they just needed meat for dinner.

Red meat was scarce and rationed, and chickens was not. Consequently, business for us skyrocketed. I remember Harry and Pete. They had been bringing live chickens to us since our store first opened. But now they had to scour all the chicken farms outside of town to bring in truckloads of live chickens to us twice a week.

It seemed like everyone had a job, and people had the money to spend. Crowds of people were walking up and down Broadway. The theaters had huge lines waiting to get a seat to see the movies. Restaurants, especially in Chinatown, had lines of customers waiting to get in. Chow Mein and deep-fried shrimp were the rage; there was a huge demand for shrimp. Pop and Mom built their business from a small store barely able to survive, to one wholesaling shrimp to Chinese restaurants. The volume sold grew from a few pounds a day to about a thousand pounds a day. Pop soon began purchasing shrimp directly from fishing boats as far away as Louisiana.

One day, while Pop was unloading a truckload of frozen shrimp at the commercial cold storage facility, he met a stranger from Mexico. The man and his brother owned several fishing boats. They fished for corbina sea bass, shrimp, and sharks for the liver that pharmaceutical manufacturers bought. This stranger was impressed by the quantity Pop was unloading---200 cases! Each case contained fifty pounds of frozen shrimp. They started a conversation that evolved into a friendly business relationship. They soon became friends, and that new friend spent many evenings having dinner at our home.

Because of this friendship, Pop was given first choice to buy from him. By this time, Pop's busines had grown large enough that he was able to buy the entire catch with cash. So, when a boat was ready to go out to sea, Pop was the first to know. He would then purchase the entire boatload, which was about 15 tons of shrimp. By the close of the shrimp season, Pop had more than 75 tons to last until the next season opened.

Our little corner store remained the same. The majority of business was conducted by telephone, and any excess supply was sent to the commercial cold storage facility. The neighbors were only aware of the retail portion of the business, and my parents preferred it that way because it was more comfortable for them to keep a low profile.

The shrimp were processed on board the ship, frozen in five-pound blocks and placed in cardboard cases, each carrying a net weight of fifty pounds. When the ship returned to port, the entire catch was loaded onto a refrigerated freight train car and sent to Nogales, Mexico, where an American customs officer would tie a seal on the door. Taxes were paid when the seal was broken. There were times when Mom would contact a buyer for the entire carload and then reroute the entire car to the purchaser. Profit was made without having to touch or even see the entire carload.

Business grew, from Pop selling as a peddler on a street corner to being a wholesaler selling more than 15 tons of fish product per month. Pop's dream became a reality when he built a building with his name on it. He was at the threshold of a new beginning at the right time. It had to do with his persistence being his own boss, despite the very hard times of the Depression.

The war brought an end to the Depression. The good times were a mixed blessing. Many homes had a little flag with a blue star in the middle hanging in their windows facing the street, letting everyone know a member of the family was fighting in the war.

I was thirteen years old, and all I knew was the war effort at home and how the news portrayed the fighting in Europe and in Asia. Other than going to school and helping out at our store, life continued naturally. I remembered that brief period when everyone was doing whatever he or she could to help in the war effort. Anyone willing to work had employment. Life for minorities improved, because people were busy working and had no time to notice the differences between each other, and racial discrimination was not an overt issue.

1927
Pop and Mom wedding photo
Pop age 31 and Mom age 22

1970
Pop age 74 and Mom age 65

CHAPTER 11
JUNIOR HIGH SCHOOL YEARS

MY graduating class, summer 1941, from 9TH Street School went to La Fayette Jr. High. For the first time, I could choose some of my classes. I chose drafting for one of my electives because my mind was set on becoming an engineer. The assignments in drafting were so easy that I completed the teacher's study plan before mid-semester. He ran out of assignments for me and tried to make up more difficult drawings to slow me down, but he could not keep up with me. Back then, I knew nothing about drafting. I was only twelve years old. The grownups around me had no professional experience. They were either laborers or family run business owners. There was no helpful experience I could relate to.

Why didn't the teacher show us the tools we needed to become drafts-men? Even something as simple as reading the label on a special pencil so that we could intelligently select the right hardness of the lead on our pencils. No! He just had us copy simple drawings he had hung along the wall.

Math class was adding, subtracting, and multiplying. I had learned that in elementary school! The closest thing to learning English was called "social events." They were trying to teach us to read the newspaper. But I had been doing that at home before going to junior high. What about grammar? I wanted to learn more about sentence construction. But that was not in the curriculum. The shortcomings in that school hurt me academically. They did not offer me any challenging subjects. The students were predominately Black and Hispanic, and it seemed the teachers did not have the will to help us. They felt we were not smart enough to deserve better schooling.

It did not take long for me to realize that some teachers were prejudiced against us. No homework was assigned. It seemed like the way to receive an" A" for the semester was to be obedient. Scholastic achievement was secondary. Gang fights were common. We had at least one every year.

The last straw for me happened in the eighth grade. The school board sent a counselor to interview each of us and help us set a course for a career. I was called into his office. I sat down, wondering what this interview was about.

What do you want to be when you grow up? He asked.

I want to be an engineer, I replied.

Without looking at me. he said,

You will never make it.

Oh yes, I will! I answered loudly.

Your math is not good enough! he said to me sarcastically.

At that moment, even as a thirteen-year-old, I thought:

How can he say that? They are not teaching anything but adding and subtracting!

I was mad, but I didn't argue with him. I just said:

I will go to summer school.

Without a word to me, he pulled out a file and read it. He was silent. Not one word of encouragement was said to me. I was mad and walked out of his office without his permission.

That evening, I told Mom I wanted to go to another school, but she said we lived in the La Fayette school district, so they would not let me attend a school in another school district.

Then she had an idea. We had a relative who owned a small grocery store just over the district boundary. We could use that address and tell them we had moved and now lived there. But if they found out, I would be ordered to return to La Fayette.

OK! Mom, I will do it, I pledged.

Mom agreed. No one would know I did not live within John Adams Junior High School district, as long as I kept quiet.

I would go to John Adams Junior High. It cost seven cents to ride the streetcar. I got there by taking the "S" car, then transferring to the "J" car.

There were a few Chinese families that lived within the John Adams Junior High School district. I was just another Chinese student in the schoolyard, so I did not attract any attention. When I transferred there in the ninth grade, I was terribly behind in math and English grammar. History and geography were no problem. Those subjects always fascinated me, and on Saturdays, I would go to the public library and read the children's history and geography books. Unfortunately, to this day, I am weak in English grammar, particularly expressing my inner feelings in writing. But math, particularly the concept of algebra, was a huge hurdle to overcome. I was at the bottom of the class because I was not interested in the mechanics of solving the problems. I wanted to understand the theory. I spent all my time trying to understand the applications of algebra. Consequently, I did not practice the mechanics of the equations. I did not develop enough accuracy to score well on quizzes. I spent all my time looking for the meaning of the problem that was delivered, like a narrative in literature. Besides, I was not concerned about being the top scorer in my class.

One day, my homeroom teacher made an offer to the class. She would give up her lunchtime to help anyone who wanted extra help in math. I took the opportunity and spent many lunchtimes trying to solve problems using algebra. The math teacher was impressed, and I received a C instead of a D for the semester. The entire year at John Adams Junior High was filling the void of poor schooling I had received at La Fayette Junior High.

My math deficiency lasted through my first semester in high school. I kept trying to break the mental barrier that kept me from understanding algebra. Then one day in summer school, while I was studying Algebra 3, it suddenly came to me. I felt like a door had opened and all the lights were suddenly turned on. I was seeing a new world I never imagined existed. From that time on, studying was easier because I was able to understand the teacher completely. This was in the second half of the tenth grade.

Socially, back when I was in the ninth grade at John Adams Jr, High, I began to meet other boys who were growing up in a more upbeat environment. During physical education period, I happened to be standing next to a boy in gym class. He told me his name was Richard Wu.

Wu? That is a Chinese name! You don't look Chinese, I said to him with a surprised look on my face.

My father is Chinese, and my mother is white. he calmly replied.

What do you call yourself? I asked.

I am American. He answered with a proud look on his face.

I had known some playmates who were half Chinese and another race. But they were part of our community and were thought of as Chinese. When Richard said he was American, it was not the answer I expected. I began to focus on his parents. He must have had an extraordinary mother to have instilled such a pride in who he is.

A boy named David and I were chatting. He told me while he was with Richard one day, the subject of religion had come up. David looked straight into my face and exclaimed:

We were talking about Sunday services. Then Richard did something I was unprepared for. He reached into his pocket and gave me his pocket-size Bible. He wouldn't take anything from me.

The boys I met on that school campus were different than those at La Fayette. They were not burdened by negativity. At La Fayette, everyone knew the hurdle that prevented them from freely achieving a good life, but at John Adams, the minority students I met were optimistic about their future. They were part of the student body that believed that the future belonged to them. Although in later life they could experience prejudice treatment in their adult life, for now, the message meant for the majority white population in school rubbed off on them.

Whether Asian, Hispanic, or Black kids, they came from homes that were not burdened with hopelessness. It seemed their parents were able to earn a decent wage or income and they provided their children with a decent foundation to begin a better life than most poorer families.

I remember one boy with red hair, blue eyes, and a happy disposition. Many times, he sang out loud in Spanish. I asked him where he learned those Mexican songs:

I am Mexican, he replied.

You don't look Mexican, I exclaimed.

I know, but I am Mexican, he said smiling with pride.

Joe Kinda was another boy I met at John Adams Jr. High. He told me about his heritage. Particularly about the Magyars, his ancestors that came from some place near Western China. Joe was a very friendly. He enjoyed talking about subjects he heard about from his father when he was growing up in Hungary. There was an air of pride in his stories about the kinship his ancestors had with the Mongolian race of that part of Asia Minor. I was thirteen years old and fascinated with what he told me. We were just casual friends who met in jr. high and that friendship grew during my high school years. Our relationship is still alive; it has been going on for 79 years. This is the year 2021. We are both 91 years old. Joe's birthday is in June, and mine is in May. He is just a few weeks younger than me.

CHAPTER 12
A NEW ADVENTURE

This was my first day in high school. Everything was new to me, the schoolyard, the buildings and the many unfamiliar faces before me as I walked through the gate onto the school ground. There were so many interesting things for me to become acquainted with. I wanted to be a part of this environment. As I slowly ventured into this unfamiliar scene, one thought hung heavy on my mind. How will I fit in?

My first encounter with white students happened when I transferred to John Adams Jr. High. I had only one year there, and it was not enough time for me to become accustomed to them. As I walked through the gate of John H. Francis Polytechnic High School, I was very reserved and kept to myself for fear of being treated as unwanted by the predominate white students. I was not sure how they would accept me socially. Although, there were some Hispanics, Asians, and Blacks on the campus, about ten percent of the school population, still, it did not dawn on me that this was my opportunity to readjust my attitude and learn how to survive outside of my minority neighborhood. All I knew was how we were restricted to where we could live and how our kind was prevented from having an unlimited future for success. I felt unsure of how I should conduct myself with strangers. Most of these students were from homes whose parents did not want us in their neighborhoods. Then, Sam appeared. He was an old neighborhood friend, another Asian. What a relief, ---someone I could relate to. That was reassuring that I was not alone.

Looking back to the year 1944, there were other instances away from my high school life I can now enjoy as humorous. We were suddenly venturing into the unknown world of the white majority. This happened during my first year of high school on a Saturday away from school.

Six of us from our neighborhood, all Chinese kids, decided to have lunch at Clifton's Cafeteria on Broadway downtown. The financial good times were just beginning, and we were trying out new adventures, ones that we could afford and feel welcomed in. Clifton's was the place. The decorations insides of the dining area were most pleasant. It felt like being on a storybook vacation island somewhere in some faraway place. The island food and the ambience were different from our ethnic culture. I remember the comfortable feeling of being in one of the few places minorities could go to and not feel unwanted.

My friends and I joined the line of patrons, picking out our choices. Then as we reached the end of the food counter, large wedges of watermelons, about one eighth of a whole one, caught our eyes. So, we each took one. We paid for our food and picked out a table to sit and eat. Without a second thought, we lifted the watermelon with both hands, ready to chomp into it like we always did at home. Suddenly, we noticed other people using forks and eating it in a genteel manner. We slowly turned and faced each other with an embarrassed feeling and sudden realization that we were acting like we had no proper upbringing. So, we copied them. We slowly placed our watermelon back on our plates, this time eating it with our forks. Everything went ok until we came to the seeds. Then reality set in. We couldn't spit out the seeds, like we did at home. We could read each other's faces. *What do we do we do? How do we get past the seeds? Just leave a good portion of it uneaten.* That was better than looking like we were brought up in a barn.

That episode was just the beginning of my growing up as a teenager into a more mature and genteel life.

Another time, I remember when Nancy called me by telephone.

Rodney! I need someone to take me to the high school achievement award dinner. Can you help me?

Both Nancy and I were from the same Chinese neighborhood. She lived on Towne Avenue, the next block from Crocker Street. We both expected the dinner to be just a simple one, like at home. Then we saw the dinner rolls.

How do you eat this? You can't bite into it like a sandwich, she commented.

I was just as puzzled as she was. We were accustomed to eating Chinese style and had never seen a dinner roll before, especially one shaped almost like a little football with a hard crust.

We looked at each other.

Let's not touch it, I suggested.

All our lives, we had been told: watch your behavior. Do not shame your family. So, there we were. The only Chinese at the dinner, bewildered and afraid to look uncultured before all those white people.

A more serious event happened in my social studies class one day. One student raised his hand to speak.

I heard that the Chinese keep their animals inside their homes to keep warm on cold nights. He said with an "I am better than they" attitude.

The teacher replied.

Yeah. And they probably sleep with them.

He Laughed as if it was a hilarious put-down remark. The class laughed with him, sharing his "we are better than they" are attitude. It was a momentary incident; then he continued his class lesson, as if his remark was just a joke at the expense of someone unable to fight back. I wanted to shout out to the teacher, especially to that boy. I wanted to say something bad back to them, but I didn't, for fear of being ganged up on by the majority of the white classmates. Besides, there is this tradition in Chinese culture: the teacher is a very respected person. No Chinese student would ever show disrespect to him. Also, common sense reminded me that I was the smallest one in class. There was no possibility for me to win a fight. So, I just sat in my seat thinking: That boy must come from a narrow-minded home, and the teacher is no better.

After class, I let it leave my mind. Why fight over something beyond my control. This was my first year in high school. I did not want to blame nor hold a grudge against every white kid on the campus. Besides, we Chinese were few as compared to the entire student body.

In a way, all that happened during my first year in high school helped me learn how to cope with real life. Those incidences were not entirely a surprise. I had been exposed to life as a minority from as far back as I could remember. Like most people, I learned how to survive by avoiding encounters that could trigger unpleasantness from an adversary. Also, I saw how my parents conducted themselves.

My mother grew up when Chinese were treated as undesirables. She lived during those times when to avoid unpleasantness, they would conduct themselves before the white community as portrayed in movies and cartoons.

She was fluent in Chinese and English. She also knew enough Spanish to understand the language. Yet, when a white person spoke to her, she replied in pigeon English.

Oh! Papa San, not here. Gone get coffee. Be back later.

"Papa San" or "Mama San" is not even an expression spoken among Chinese. It was how the entertainment industry portrayed us. But Mom used it to survive in a hostile world.

I hated it when she lowered herself like that. I was in my early teens, and I was beginning to feel that life could be better if I did not allow myself to be treated as an inferior person.

I said to my mother:

Mom, you speak good English. They have no respect for you. Show them you are better than how they want you to be. Don't let them put you down.

I wanted her to stand up, be proud and fight back. She quietly listened to me. Said nothing. Mom knew I was right. But it was not easy for her to change. She grew up in a different time, when that was the safest way to survive. I understood and said no more.

CHAPTER 13
BRIDGING THE CULTURAL GAP

On the school grounds, the demeaning experiences I had experienced from my childhood days hung over my head like a cloud. I did not want to provoke any displeasure. I felt insecure. How would they treat me? One wrong behavior could justify their negative perception about me.

In reality, all the students cared about were the classes available and the challenges of the subjects they were about to study. My presence on campus made no impact socially. No one seemed engrossed in social issues.

It didn't take long for me to notice; most students came from different ethnic backgrounds. I didn't know that. I thought all white folks were the same. My biggest discovery was the Mexicans. I knew them as minorities like me. Yet, I couldn't tell them apart from the other students. They behaved no different than other students on campus. Another group I thought I knew were the Jews. My views about them were influenced by the negative perception voiced by some of the people on San Pedro Street. Thinking back to those days, I realize it was a part of the everyday life when many had not yet learned to live together with those who are different.

Some of the white students were first generation in America. They were from all parts of Europe, including the Middle East. Some had relatives back from where they came from, like many of my people. It was then I discovered, I was not alone in this struggle to become American.

School had just let out. John and I were both walking to the corner to catch the streetcar, just talking, nothing important. He mentioned:

I'm Armenian.

That was the first time I had heard of that group.

You know how to tell when someone is Armenian? Look at his last name. Most Armenian names end with ian, he added.

Another time, I was on the schoolyard with Hans. I remember that he said to me:

My mother and father are from Germany. My older brother stayed behind and is in the German army.

A thought ran through my mind. "*We are at war with Germany, and part of his family is on the enemy side.*"

I began to realize, quite a few had come from families still living the culture of a foreign nation and in the process of becoming American.

One day, Walter Epstein and I were having a casual conversation as we were going for lunch. Walt told me he was joining a demonstration against a speaker in our auditorium on Saturday.

Why? I asked.

That speaker is known to be anti-Semitic and is very outspoken against Jews, he said.

That was the first time I had heard about public speakers. Walter was white and Jewish. Yet, he felt the same kind of discomfort I had when I was away from my neighborhood friends.

My perception of the students began to slowly change, not suddenly, but gradually as I got to know them.

I didn't know it then, but later in my adult life, I realized that friendship start when both parties have at least one or two values in common.

CHAPTER 14
HIGH SCHOOL MEMORIES

Gosh, the memories of the good old days in high school sure bring back nostalgic feelings. I can still picture that time when school had just let out. I was walking along the sidewalk with a group of friends, coming up to the most dangerous driveway to catch the streetcar. Just as we neared that driveway, everyone stopped talking. We had to pay attention to the cars racing out of the dirt parking lot. The boys are driving out like they had just left the starting line of a race, showing off their driving skill.

RRRR, RRRR, SCREECH, SCREECH!

Their wheels were burning rubber on the pavement as the hotrods raced out with a jump-start from the parking lot. None of those drivers ever gave a thought to safety for pedestrians. How no one got hurt was a miracle. We stood by, amidst all the dust kicked up by the hotrods. Those were the days. We loved every bit of it.

I can still picture how when someone lifted up the hood, we would crowd around his car and gasp.

Look at that shiny silver engine, two carburetors and two exhaust pipes. Bet he could do 90 miles an hour! one of the boys said.

Some of the guys ran out of money before they could finish rebuilding their cars. My friend Ronald was one of them. He ran out of money before he could fix the speedometer.

I had an old used Oldsmobile Mom had bought for me. It must have been at least ten years old. But everything worked. So, he asked me,

Hey, Rodney, can you help me find out how fast my car can go?

Sure, what do you want me to do? I asked.

Drive along side of me and tell me how fast I am going, he replied.

OK! I answered.

So, I raced down the neighborhood street shouting.

You are doing 30, now 40.

How we avoided an accident I don't know.

As I thought back to those days, I decided to telephone my best old friend, Joe Kinda. We are now 91 years old. Not too many friends left to talk about those good old days.

Hi! Joe, how are you? I spoke.

Well, I am still on the right side of the grass, he said.

Laughing as he joked. Then we started talking about our high school days.

Rodney! Do you remember our buddy Hal Bishop? Wonder if he is still around. Haven't heard from him since graduation, Joe said.

I really enjoyed reliving those days as Joe continued.

Remember when Hal was building a hotrod from an old model B Ford and ran out of money before completing it? You and I were passengers. The car had no brakes. Hal drove slowly, so when he had to stop, he would shift to reverse, hoping he wouldn't strip his gears.

I got so engrossed with our conversation that before Joe could finish talking, I interrupted and said,

Then you and I would stand up in the car waving our arms and shouting to anyone in front of us. No brakes! No brakes!

Later, after we hung up, I thought back to when Joe and I were together in the land surveying class. No other high school offered land surveying, but Poly did. We were very fortunate to have Mr. Lorraine as our teacher. He taught us surveying on the college level. I still remember his story about when he was on his way to Alaska and met this young lady in Pasadena and married her.

Lucky for us, he decided to become an instructor at Poly High School. I remember how proud he was of his past students. He often mentioned how successful they were as professional surveyors with just the training they got from his class.

Joe, Hal and I made a three men survey crew, and we performed a lot line survey on the school yard, just the way Mr. Lorraine taught us.

That reminded me about my problem with Joe and Hal. I was 5 feet 2 and Joe was 6 feet tall, and Hal must have been about 6-4. Every so often, they set the tripod legs so I couldn't reach the eye piece on the transit.

Doggone you guys. Couldn't you lower the legs a little, so I can have a chance? I complained.

Then either Joe or Hal would reply with a stern voice.

Look! We have a class assignment to do. So quit squawking. Go get that trash can over there and turn it upside down, so you can stand on it. Well! What are you waiting for?

Boy! Was I mad! There was nothing I could do about it, but what they said.

One day, I was over at Joe's house celebrating his 90th birthday. His family was there, including grandchildren. Joe and I started talking about our experience learning land surveying at Poly. He started laughing.

Do you remember how mad you got when you couldn't reach the eye piece on the transit? You never figured out that it happened whenever we were near trash can. Joe said with a huge smile on his face.

Then it dawned on me. They purposely wanted to see me mad, so they could scold and tell me to quit complaining.

Those were the days Joe and I never tired talking about.

Another time, when I visited Joe at his home, we talked about a time during lunch break. I remember every bit of it. Joe brought up the subject.

Remember when we were walking past the gym and read the note on the door inviting anyone to join the wrestling competiton? I talked you into joining.

That brought back memories. After school, Joe went to the "Y" to practice wrestling. I had to go to Chinese school, but I was strong and felt I could win a few matches. Besides, this was a good opportunity to beat up some guys without them getting mad at me. So, I signed up.

After losing a string of matches, my next opponent was a Japanese fellow. He was smaller than me.

Boy! Am I gonna win this one! I said to myself.

The match started, and I grabbed hold of him. I was just about to toss him on the mat, when suddenly, ***wham!*** He threw me on the floor. I didn't know he had been going to judo school! That guy knew ju-jitsu! I tell you, every time I hit the floor, I saw stars.

Joe went on to win the championship, and I had the unbroken record of defeats.

CHAPTER 15
FISHING WITH JOE

Every year from the mid 1970's to the early 1990's, just after the ice on the rivers began to melt in the Arctic, Joe and I flew to a fishing lodge in either Alaska or Canada. What a great vacation. Just us and a group of men roughing it in the wild.

Some roughing it! We flew to Edmonton in Canada by commercial airline and waited for a private plane to take us to the lodge on Great Bear Lake in the Northwest Territory. There were ten of us. The private plane from the lodge waited for us at the Edmonton airport. As I approached for boarding, the first thing I noticed was the mud splash on the tail end. I was a little worried, but didn't give it much thought. When we arrived, I saw the muddy landing field. Oh well! We landed safely.

Gary, one of our friends, began to rub mosquito repellant lotion on himself.

Going to put on enough of this repellant so the mosquitoes will just slide off me,

he said laughingly. Seriously, though, mosquitoes were plentiful there. Sometimes, clouds of them were flying in the air.

The lodge had two beds to a room---all rooms were heated and contained the comforts of any modern hotel. The dining room looked like a high-end restaurant. There was no menu; everyone got the same meals. Great food! While we ate breakfast, Native Indian guides waited for us in a small boat outfitted with an outboard motor and fishing gear. That was roughing it in luxury.

No need to for an alarm clock to wake us up for breakfast. *The men from the other rooms were banging on the doors!*

Let's go fishing! The men shouted as they walked down the hallway.

Our guide waited for us in a boat large enough for him and two passengers. Everything was ready for fishing. Joe and I got into the boat and sat down. Then, the Indian guide started the outboard motor and took us out to the deep water. The fishing was catch and release. When we caught a fish, the guide wouldn't let us haul it in. He took over and lifted the fish up by its head and gently removed the hook. Then the guide would hold up the lake trout and say "**seven pounds**" or whatever he estimated. After that, he carefully revived the fish and set it free. This was a necessary conservation act. The fishing was great, never a dull moment. Come lunch time, the guide would say:

Keep the little one for lunch.

Then we landed on an island. He cleaned the fish, wrapped it with aluminum foil together with slices of lemon and some fruit and vegetables and cooked it on an open fire. Now, how's that for roughing it in the wild?

The other guests were from parts of Canada and New England, besides us from California. After dinner, a few lounged on comfortable sofas socializing. Others played poker. But the activity that amazed me were the guys watching the videos. They never got tired watching films of someone hauling in a large trout. Every episode was the same. Just one catch after another. I could hear them shouting.

Wow, look at that catch!

The moment I enjoyed the most was when the lodge manager called us together to hear who had caught the largest fish. Well, when fishing is catch and release, there is no proof for honesty. The biggest liar is the winner. It was fun. No one really believed the others. We just laughed at their stories.

The next day, the weather suddenly changed. Strong winds were blowing, causing rough water with high waves. The manager of the lodge did not want us out on the lake.

*I can't let you out on the lake until the wind dies down, h*e announced to us.

Why? shouted a few men.

It's too dangerous. The waves are too high. Besides, you wouldn't be able to fish! he replied.

Look, we came here to go fishing. Why should we let a little storm stop us? shouted one of the men.

OK! OK! But, it's at your own risk. I will have a guide help you the best he can. The rest of you stay here and be comfortable, he warned.

He expected only a few who spoke up to walk out. You should have seen the look on his face when everyone got up and walked out to their little fishing boats. No one wanted to look chicken.

Gosh. It was dangerous. I saw waves that could sink us. Luckily, no one got washed into the lake. On top of that foolishness, we couldn't cast our lines out to the water. Just as suddenly as the wind started, it stopped. So, happily we fished, satisfied that we beat the odds. We showed the manager we were men. It was a bit juvenile for successful businessmen, but what the heck. We had something to brag about

Another year, we flew to a different lodge near the Arctic Circle. I wanted to try out my light fishing gear. It was brand new. I had wanted to use it to catch Arctic graylings. But I caught something that fought hard to get free. We were fishing at the mouth of a stream feeding the lake.

Joe, I got a bite! I shouted.

I was ready for an exciting fight from the fish when suddenly, I heard the sound.

Crack!

I sat in our little boat with just the handle of my pole remaining in my grip.

Another year, Joe and I joined a group going to Alaska to fish. We were going after halibut in Homer. There were at least sixteen guys with only one thought in mind. Catch the big one. I baited my large hook with a chunk of octopus. It must have been a half pound! Everyone dropped their lines in the water and waited.

I got a tug on my line. It was a heavy tug. I got a huge one—the largest caught by anyone. I reeled him in. Then the skipper of the boat threw a gaffing hook tied to a rope overboard and hooked the halibut. It took two guys to help me get the ninety-pound fish onto the boat.

Everyone joined me celebrating at the bar. I had to pay because I had won the jackpot. The drinks cost me more than I won! I think the guys had more fun getting free drinks than admiring me for the catch. But I had a great time, and it was worth it.

After the drinks, I couldn't wait—I had to call home. Joy answered the phone. Without saying who I was. I shouted:

I caught a ninety-pound halibut!

There is something about being out in the open, away from the city, relaxing and experiencing the challenge of bringing in a fish. Most of the time, we only sat in the boat, the two of us, Joe and I, saying nothing to each other and enjoying the solitude and fresh air. We understood each other. The reward was, of course, the fish we caught and could talk about.

One day at Joe's home, we spent time talking about the good old days. Joe mentioned the fun times he and his family had been fishing in Panguich, Utah. So, we decided to spend a few days at the lake there. His son and another friend came along. No fish were biting. We just lulled on our boat with our lines hopelessly dangling in the water trying to catch at least one trout. Joe's son. Donald, a typical young twenty-year old, was bored. He was lying on the seat of the boat facing the water and jokingly saying,

Here, fishy, fishy, fishy.

Like calling for a dog to come. It was something a young fellow would do when bored to death. We were pretty far from the shore, and you might think our voices could not be heard that far away. But when we came in for the day, a man greeted us with a grin on his face, and jokingly said:

I heard you guys calling for the fish to come to your boat.

I had a client who owned a lodge near Lake Panguich. He offered free lodgings for me and a guest of my choice. Naturally, I asked Joe, and he invited his brother and another friend. When we got there, clouds were in the sky. It looked like rain. We looked at each other.

We came this far to fish. And besides, we only have three days to enjoy ourselves. Let's go, Joe said.

So, we rented a boat and headed out. There we were, four old guys in an aluminum boat in the middle of Lake Panquich. It began to thunder, and lightning could be seen on the horizon. We were a bunch of crazy guys fishing in the rain. If we'd been struck by lightning, we could have been fried! Barbecued! And we didn't catch anything.

It sure was nice reuniting with Joe. It brought back good memories. I wondered how the other guys I had known in high school were doing, Hal, Lucky, and a few others. The next morning, I went out front to pick up the newspaper. There was an article that caught my attention about a festival somewhere in San Bernardino, near the freeway to Lake Arrowhead. The reporter mentioned one of the vendors was "outspoken and colorful." It was Lucky! I had known him in high school. Joe grew up with him. I immediately telephoned Joe.

Hey, Joe! Go out and buy the Los Angeles times. There is a story about a festival in San Bernardino, and Lucky is in it.

Joe and I hadn't heard from him since high school. We were old buddies from our teenage years. Joe looked him up, and soon the three of us were united again.

2019
Joe Kinda and Rodney

CHAPTER 16
REUNITING WITH ANOTHER OLD FRIEND

J oe kidded Lucky about the Los Angeles Times article.

What were you selling at that fair? he asked.

Cigarettes, Lucky replied.

What were you complaining about? Did you report the accurate sales amount for taxes? Joe kidded Lucky.

Of course! he replied. We laughed.

Yeah, I bet you did. Joe said.

Lucky's parents were from Oklahoma, and his father was part Native American Indian. He had blond hair and blue eyes. And I heard him say:

I am the whitest Indian around.

Lucky was a union man, a fighter for the underdog, and whenever he had a choice to patronize a white-owned or Black-owned store, he would always go to the Black-owned one because he wanted them to be successful. One day, he presented me with a Levi jacket and said to me,

Rodney, I saw it at some yard sale, and it looks like your size. I bought it and sent it to the cleaners. I want you to have it.

It may have been bought at a yard sale, but for me, it was the most precious gift I ever got. To this day, I still have it and will never throw it away.

Rodney wearing the jacket from Lucky

One year, Joe and I were invited to Lucky's mother's 100th birthday party. His sister told the family story, a story typical of the Great Depression.

My mother and father left Oklahoma with nothing but a donkey and a wagon. They were going to the panhandle of Texas to start a new life with barely enough food and money for survival. Pa said to Ma, "It will be lucky if we make it there."

They did and found an abandoned shack to stay in. Wind blew through the cracks, and they used old newspapers to seal them.

So, that is why they chose Lucky for the name of their first child. Soon after, the family moved to Los Angeles. Joe and I have similar beginnings. Our parents and Lucky's too worked hard and made it through the Depression. They set the foundation for our success. I like to feel that our families are the kind of people that made America.

There we were. Three very close friends, Joe, Lucky and I, a bunch of old guys, each at the prime of our lives, married, raising families and living a typical life, getting together again many years after Poly High School. Thinking back, that must have been around 1971.

Lucky suffered from diabetes and lost his legs below his knees. His health slowly deteriorated. By 1973, Lucky had passed away. It is not easy outliving old friends, but life goes on.

CHAPTER 17
HOW I MET MY FUTURE WIFE

After three years in Poly, I graduated in the summer of 1947 and went to USC to study engineering. The short time between high school graduation and college was spent searching for an answer for my future. Deep inside, I felt like I still had one foot in my ethnic neighborhood and the other foot on the doorsteps of American life. My values were changing.

I was neither a teenager nor an adult. After entering college, it dawned on me. This was the beginning of my life as an adult. My focus was on studying for a career and finding a wonderful girl. I knew most of the Chinese students at both USC and UCLA. Back then, the Chinese community was small, and most knew each other. One of them was my friend Edward. He lived near Chinatown, and I lived father South in the City Market area. We had met in Chinese school back in our high school days and became good friends while at USC. We both went to the monthly Chinese Club meetings at USC to have a good time and meet girls.

Both USC and UCLA had a Chinese Club. The meetings were held once a month and open for anyone, regardless of whether students were Chinese or not. It was a casual social event, mostly to relax and enjoy each other's company. Once in a while, someone would have a party on a Friday night at their home, and friends were invited. The invitations were verbal. The UCLA students had theirs, and we at USC had ours.

The campus cafeteria was a common place where we could run into friends and enjoy each other's company. I happened to find Edward there one day and joined him for lunch. He told me he had heard that there was to be a UCLA house party Friday.

I know where the house is, Edward said:

Henry, Edward's friend, joined us. He got interested. So, the three of us decided.

We know most of them. They won't know we're not invited. Let's go.

We crashed the party. As we entered the house, I noticed a pretty girl with some guy. I had never seen her before. I took a chance and approached her.

May I have a dance with you? I asked.

Yes, she replied.

I hadn't spent long with her when Edward called me over.

We have to leave, Edward whispered to me.

Why? We've only been here about one hour, I queried.

Henry drank too much. He's drunk, Edward said in a low voice.

I looked Edward in the face and spoke.

Edward! I just met this girl. I don't know her name! OK! I'll take a gamble and ask her for her name and telephone. Quick give me a pencil and paper.

Edward reached into his pocket. He only had an address book to write on. So, desperately, he ripped out a blank sheet and handed it to me with a pencil. I might not see her again. I had to take a chance. I asked her, hoping she wouldn't say no.

Can I have your name and telephone number? I have to leave.

It paid off. She gave me the information. I was in too much of a hurry and did not pay attention to her name. It was Joy Ruth Gray. Gray is not a Chinese name. But she looked Chinese. The next day, I called. The voice that answered had a Southern accent. It was her mother. I said:

I am Rodney, and I met Joy the other evening at the UCLA party. May I speak to her?

Joy came to the phone and I asked her if I could come visit her. She said,

Yes.

Not long after, we began spending time together, and the more I got to know Joy, the better I liked her, and we realize we were well suited for each other.

I learned she was adopted. Her mother was Cammie Gray, originally from Kansas City, Missouri. This was in the year 1951. Meanwhile, North Korea had invaded South Korea. The military draft was on, but the draft board gave me a deferment and did not call me until late 1952. Joy and I had an agreement: We would wait until I got out of the military, then marry.

CHAPTER 18

ARMY LIFE

Edward got called up before me and served on the front lines in Korea. I remained in college to complete my engineering studies. The men students at USC were largely EX-GI's from the recent war. They were very serious students and a generation ahead of me in maturity. I tried my best to keep up with them in class. It was a challenge, because my exposure to life was not as sophisticated as theirs. They were able to relate to the class subjects a lot more easily than I could.

In 1952, I graduated with a B.E. degree, and the draft board sent me a notice to report to the recruiting office, on Washington Boulevard and Hill Street. Mom wouldn't come downstairs to see me off. I am sure she didn't want me to see her in tears. So, I just shouted goodbye to her and got into Pop's truck. Pop drove me to the recruiting office. He looked very calm and said nothing. Then he made some traffic violation and was stopped by a police officer and given a citation. It was then I realized, he was upset and worried.

Several young men were there from my neighborhood. It was almost like a gathering of old friends. After we were sworn in, the bus took us to Fort Ord near Monterey. There were at least 300 of us, and basic training was fourteen weeks. Each had an assignment in the barracks, and mine was to keep the brass strainer on the long urinal clean and shinning. Some job! But I couldn't complain. I just had to figure out a plan to keep my hand out of all the piss.

Got it! I will get out of bed as fast as I can and race to the urinal before anyone gets there. Then, I'll take the shiny brass strainer out., keep it in my pocket, and replace it as soon as possible after everyone leaves for the mess hall.

Before breakfast, the sergeant had us stand at attention. He inspected everyone, making sure we were clean-shaven. Somehow, he knew most Chinese young men did not need to shave until we were well into our twenties. I was one of them. So, he instructed me to step forward to where he was able to spot any fuzz by turning my face against the sun. Sure, enough he could see the tiny fuzz that was not readily visible.

You didn't shave! Sarge barked.

But I don't have any hair on my face! I replied.

Get back in the barrack and shave that fuzz off! Sarge demanded.

Most men complained about the quality of the food, but I couldn't understand why. It sure tasted good to me. Maybe it was because I had always eaten Chinese food at home, and an American meal was a treat for me. I drank tea at home, not coffee. Breakfast was chipped ham with gravy over toast. "*Shit on the shingle*" They called it. Again, another new meal for me. I loved it.

We had a brief break after breakfast, then the whistle. Everyone rushed outside to stand in formation. Now! I had a complaint. For psychological reasons, all the short guys were in the rear, and the taller ones stood in front. The tallest guy held the platoon flag and set the pace for marching. My problem was it took one and a half of my steps to equal just one of his. I was half running all the time to keep up with the platoon. Another gripe I had was that when I was standing with the M1 rifle with the bayonet attached, the weapon was taller than me! Gosh, how would I survive in battle?

We took a class on how to survive in hand-to-hand combat, as if that one lecture was enough to make seasoned fighters of us. The instructor pointed to me. I was the smallest, and that made it easy for him to demonstrate.

He is a judo expert! Some smart ass shouted.

A judo expert? I couldn't handle a fight to save my life! But I played along. I held the bayonet in my fist and pretended I was ready to chop him in pieces. Then I asked,

Are you ready?

Uhh, go back and sit down, the instructor said.

Then he pointed to another easy victim and used him for the demonstration.

I learned a lesson the hard way. We were in bivouac pup tents. Each of us carried half a tent. I awoke very early that morning and had to take a piss. When I returned, every tent looked the same. Which was mine? Good thing I shared the tent with another guy and shouted his name. He appeared, and I was able to find my tent. What a relief. I might have had to sleep outside without a tent to protect me from the cold. Upon daylight, everyone received ammo for our M1 rifles. The sergeant called us together while a soldier sat, passing out the ammo to us.

I want everyone to recognize poison oak. Be careful, this place is full of it, he announced.

Then he pointed his finger to where this soldier was sitting.

See what he is sitting in? That is poison oak.

You should have seen the look on that guy's face. There was nothing he could do about it. He knew what poison oak would do to his skin, but we were out in the boondocks. No medic was available. All he could do was wait to see what would happen. I was sure glad it wasn't me.

I often wondered, *when are they going to teach us how to fight?* Instead, we marched in formation with continued shouting, officers reminding us constantly that they were in command. One command we constantly heard was:

You are not paid to ask questions. You just take orders!

Then, things slowly dawned on me. We were pawns in a chess game. Our lives meant nothing. We were supposed to do as ordered and try to survive the best we could while being a small part of a segment of a greater plan to win an objective. Basic training was to condition our minds to that of robots. We should just follow orders, not think as individuals. No wonder after returning to civilian life, some never readjusted. They were hopelessly lost in a world without a guiding hand.

Back in the barrack at night, the first thing that struck me was how everyone snored in different tones, like a concert. It reminded me of walking in a field at night and hearing the crickets. It was also amazing seeing guys trying to sew their emblems on their uniforms, or watching the washing machines over flow with soap suds because they were doing their laundry for the first time. Back in civilian life, they would not be caught doing this *"women's work."* Some of the men came from the deep South. One fellow hadn't readjusted and unknowingly spoke to a Black soldier insultingly. This Black man was also from the South, and at the slightest provocation, released explosive anger. That Southerner learned a lesson. This was California. He did not have the support of the multitude for his white-superior attitude and was beaten badly by the Black fellow. As I witnessed this incident, I learned a lesson. Everyone has feelings. We need to recognize it and treat others as we want others to treat us.

As I witnessed this, a thought came to my mind. There was a slogan at the recruiting office back in Los Angeles. It read something like this, not sure, though, of the exact wording: "*Through this portal everyone is equal.*" Yes! When we are fighting a common enemy. But how about when I return to civilian life? I'm not sure that rings true. I needed to just reexamine how I would feel towards someone less fortunate than me.

One evening, Lt. Ducco came over to me and asked,

How do you feel about fighting the Chinese in Korea?

I didn't appreciate his question, but kept my feelings to myself as I looked at him. I wanted to say, **your name doesn't sound very American either.** But I held back and asked,

Why should that make a difference?

CHAPTER 19

AM I GOING TO BE IN THE INFANTRY?

After we got our uniforms, we took placement exams to determine which branch of the Army we would be assigned to. I knew Cantonese Chinese as a second language, so I figured maybe I would be an interpreter. Was I surprised! I couldn't understand enough to translate from the recording. The speaker talked about ordinary happenings in America. He mentioned some well-known people.

Wah sing dun.

That was easy, Washington. Then other names were mentioned. I couldn't understand. My dilemma brought back memories of when I was ten years old and my friend Henry showed me a branch of a cotton plant. I was fascinated. That was the first time I had seen a plant with cotton growing like a flower.

Where did you get this plant? I asked.

My father's friend gave it to me. He is from Buck Gah Faay, Henry replied.

What? I asked.

Buck Gah Faay, he repeated.

Where is Buck Gah Faay? I asked.

I don't know, he said.

Several years later, I heard "***Buck Gah Faay***" again. Suddenly, I got it. It was Bakersfield. How was I supposed to make that connection? That was how I felt listening to the recording. Then there was another problem. He spoke in very proper Cantonese Chinese. The only Cantonese I knew was brought over to America a long time ago from the villages. Some of the phrases were no longer used in China. The Chinese language school I attended taught literature, Chinese history, and the geography of China, not proper grammar.

My memories kept returning. One time my wife and I were sitting in a restaurant in Chinatown, San Francisco. A young lady shared the table with us. We started to get acquainted. She asked,

What dialect do you speak?

Chung Shan, I answered.

Oh! You are one of those Chinese hillbillies, she replied.

What do you speak? I asked.

Sze Yup.

We always thought you Sze Yups were the backwards ones, I said with a smile.

We had a good laugh together. Yes, I understood the village version of Cantonese Chinese, but that person on that test recording spoke proper standard Cantonese. No wonder I couldn't follow his conversation. So, I flunked.

Signal Corps was another option.

OK! Men, the monitor said.

This is "A", dot dash. Got it?

This is "H", dot dot dot dot.

There was one more letter in the Morse code. Then he asked:

Are you ready?

That was easy. Just those three letters? Maybe I have a chance to be in the Signal Corps.

Then the test began. Dot dot dot dash dot--- it was so fast. I couldn't make sense of it. The heck with it. I threw my pencil onto the floor. It sure looked like I would be in the infantry. The next day was the interview.

You qualify for officer's training school. Will you accept? The interviewer asked.

Hell no! I answered.

Why not? he asked.

I am not brave and tough enough to lead a group of men into combat, I replied.

As I said that, one thought ran through my mind: I am not going to be like Teddy Roosevelt, leading the charge up San Juan Hill against a hail of bullets. I want to be the last and slowest running up that hill.

OK, he said,

Then you have to sign this paper acknowledging your refusal.

I signed it eagerly. Now, I was sure they would assign me to the infantry. I wasn't good enough for those other specialties. That's life. I tried, but failed. Oh, well!

The next day, I had another interview. I sat down and waited to hear my fate. This guy would let me know what part of the Army I would be assigned to. He looked at me and said:

You are classified SPP, Scientific and Professional Personal.

What? I refused an opportunity to be an officer, and I get in a noncombat unit? Huh? Well! I guess if I had accepted the offer to go to officer's training school, they would have sent me to the infantry. Whew!

Out of over 300, only three of us were chosen SPP. The next morning, the captain made an announcement before dismissing us for breakfast.

We have a few geniuses in our company, he said and read out only two Caucasian names. I was not included.

Did they change their mind about me? I went to the office and asked the clerk about my assignment. He read the list. I was on it. Then I realized the captain did not want to recognize me as one of those "*geniuses*" he mentioned. I was sure glad I was not going to serve under him in combat.

My orders were to report to Fort Lee, Virginia. I was in the fourth week of basic training and did not have to complete the remaining ten weeks.

The farthest North I had ever traveled up to that time was San Francisco. The farthest East was to Las Vegas, and the farthest South, Tijuana, Mexico. My Army travel itinerary took me first to Chicago, then on another train to St. Petersburg, Virginia. I had no idea what to do but just followed instructions blindly until I reached my destination.

Just as I got off the train at St. Petersburg, I saw a sign on the door that read "*white*." A sign on the other door read "*colored*." I had heard about Jim Crow laws before, but it was my first time being confronted with them. This unnerved me, because I was afraid that they might also treat me badly. It was difficult enough being a minority in California. But at least I was not blatantly treated like this.

What do I do? There is no door for Chinese or Asians. I didn't come this far just to get into trouble.

So, I threw my duffle bag on my shoulders and walked around the train station and got into the waiting bus that took me to Fort Lee.

CHAPTER 20
WAITING FOR AN ASSIGNMENT

I finally arrived at Fort Lee, where the sleeping quarters were permanent two-story masonry buildings. There must have been at least 100 men in this huge room with double bunk beds.

Our group of fifty was temporarily sharing the room with them. They were waiting for discharge. Many of those men were recovering from battle injuries.

It seemed like the administration did not know what to do with us. We had been investigated and received preliminary clearance. Fort Lee was just the temporary holding place for us until we received top-secret clearance. They kept us in the dark, and we had no idea what we would be doing.

Fortunately, when I was in high school, then college, my focus was to be an engineer. Who would have guessed that that schooling opened the door for me to be in this part of the Army? The belief in my neighborhood was that we minorities would never be able to rise up in positions of importance without a good education. Our parents kept urging us to continue past high school onto college. It was because of my education that I was assigned SPP, doing something important.

The men in my group were all college graduates. Many had Master's and PhD degrees. I was one of the few with only a bachelor's degree. They were worldly in thought and more tolerant than some I knew from my childhood days. Those men came from all over America, and because of the comradery I had with them in the barracks, I began to feel like I belonged. I was becoming one of them, an American.

There were fifty of us SPP's. Each was a college graduate in the sciences. We spent the day lolling around in the library or taking walks around the base. This is where I met Andrew Cook. He came from Glendale near Griffith Park in Los Angeles. We were both interested in the architectural magazines showing house plans. Our thoughts were that some day when we became successful, we would build the house of our dreams. It was just something to talk about, since there was nothing else to do. Once in a while, we were given some mundane task.

Most of the men were typical scholarly no-nonsense college students with one objective in mind, get an education in their chosen field. Among us were a few with little social maturity. I remember Jacob. He spent his time buried in his studies and probably had never even kissed a girl, let alone dated one. We called him *"Dad Jacobs."* He was the stereotypical scholar---glasses, short, chubby---the kind most girls would find boring. Walter came from a wealthy family and talked a big story about his exploits with women. He sounded like he had a carefree life with no concern about his future. Whenever, he talked about the women in his life, no one cared to listen, but "Dad" was fascinated with Walter's bragging. So, he asked Walter,

How did you find these women?

It's easy, just go to a bar, and you'll find someone. Chat with her and offer to buy her a drink, Walter replied.

About a week later, our orders came through. The Department of Agriculture wanted some statistics on what percentage of meat was actually consumed by the soldiers. This was only a temporary assignment to keep us busy until we received top secret clearance. We were to travel to various Army camps by a special train, a Pullman car, and two porters came along to change our bed sheets and give us the typical royal treatment that came with the train ticket. The project was named the Boneless Beef study. We were to spend one week at a company mess hall, record the weight of beef before it was cooked, then weigh the scraps the men would throw into the garbage. Several times, there would be a layover to connect our car to another train going to our destination.

When we reached Memphis, Tennessee, the train disconnected our pullman car for a two-day layover. That evening, Stan and I stayed in our car while the others went into town to see the sights. It was late in the evening. Dad Jacobs entered the car breathless and panting.

What happened? we asked.

You look like you have been running.

Do you remember when I was talking with Walter, and he told me how to meet up with a girl? Well, I did. I did just what Walter told me. She invited me to her apartment. She told me to relax while she went to her bathroom to change out of her street clothes. I sat down, started thinking, and the more I thought, the more scared I got. Then I lost my nerve, got off her sofa, and bolted out of her apartment before she reappeared. I just ran and ran and ran until I got here.

So, that ended our first episode of traveling with scholarly unsophisticated bookworms.

Whenever we reached an Army camp, we held a letter from some high command that placed us out of reach of any camp commander. The lieutenant in charge was another college graduate with no respect for Army procedures. There were several instances when we were challenged for our lack of military discipline. We managed to arrive on time at the mess hall and did our job, but observed no military decorum. The career officers tried to exert pressure on us to make us behave like soldiers, but couldn't.

Another time, we went to a camp in West Virginia. We were going to dinner at the mess hall. Everyone with a tray in hand walked in line as the servers scooped portions onto our trays. I was just like the rest of them, getting dinner, when this tall guy saw me. He was serving mashed potatoes with a long-handled scoop. He had never been out of the hills in West Virginia and had never seen a real live Asian; he had only seen us in movies. He got very excited, and with the long-handled scoop in his hand, pointed it toward my face and shouted,

I know what you are! I seen you in movies! Then plop, plop, I got two scoops instead of one.

Fort Leonard Wood near Waynesville, Missouri, was our next destination. We arrived a little early on Friday. That gave us a three-day weekend. One of the fellows mentioned Panama City and wanted to see the beach resort town. So, about fifteen of us decided to hitchhike from Fort Leonard Wood. We decided to go in twos or threes, so we could have a better chance of getting rides. We were spread out standing along the highway. The plan was the first ones reaching the beach would get a motel room and wait until everyone arrived. We would flip a coin to see who got the mattress, the box spring, and who had to sleep on the floor.

Gregg and another guy finally arrived, the last ones. As Gregg approached us, he gave a warning.

Don't anyone make any wise cracks, or I will let you have it.

Hey! What's the problem? one guy asked.

You'll see, Gregg answered.

We stepped out of the door, and there were two women in a car waiting. They had picked up Gregg and Jim and wanted to spend the night with us. They looked like prostitutes. None of us wanted anything to do with them.

How do we get rid of them? Gregg muttered.

Let's all of us leave for dinner and not pay attention to them. That should give them the message, Jim suggested.

It worked. When we returned to the motel, they were gone. Now we could better spend what little time we had to enjoy a tourist retreat most of us would not have had the opportunity to see otherwise.

We had a longer stay than usual in Missouri, giving us an opportunity to see the Ozarks. Four of us somehow ended up along a meadow close to a stream. We went over to it and saw a sign on the other side. It was too far away, and we couldn't read it.

Wonder what it says, one fellow mused.

Yeah, why don't we swim across and find out, another guy suggested.

The water had a strong current, and I didn't want to swim against the flow. Besides, none of us had swimming trunks.

Let's swim on a diagonal heading against the current. We should land right in front of the sign, the other guy said.

So, they striped off their clothes and swam naked to read the sign. I wouldn't follow. It was a tough fight going against the flow of the water, but they made it and swam back.

What did the sign say? I asked.

Private property. Keep out, one guy replied with a sigh.

They could have been swept away by the strong current and drowned. Oh well! They may have been college educated. But that didn't mean they were mature enough to not take chances like that.

We had gone to several different camps across the southerly states from Alabama through Arizona. While we were in Alabama, the train had a short stop over, so we went into the train depot for lunch. One of the men with us, Arthur, was Black. He was a mathematician, PhD, and professor at UC Berkeley. The waiter at the dinner told the lieutenant Arthur could not eat in the same room with the rest of us. He had to eat in the other room by himself. None of us were from the South and were unprepared for this. The lieutenant uncomfortably told Arthur to go into the next room to eat.

Arthur was one of us. Up to then, no one saw him as different. Everyone wanted to do something about it. But we couldn't. We felt awful and helpless. No one wanted to talk about it. We just continued on our travel with no mention of this ever happening.

The train had a six-hour stopover in Albuquerque, New Mexico. About six of the guys, including the lieutenant in charge, decided to see the town. The rest of the guys stayed on the train and relaxed. Amazingly, the six made it back in time, so drunk they could barely walk. Each one helped the others, including the lieutenant who was supposed to keep military discipline. That was lucky because our Pullman had been hitched onto another train ready to leave with a schedule they were determined to keep.

Finally, when we reached Camp Roberts in California, our top-secret clearance came through. We stayed there for a few weeks waiting for new instructions from whatever headquarters was keeping track of us. A few of us got a three-day pass to go home for a short visit. Our assignment was still a mystery to us. We were instructed to go to a place just outside of Baltimore, Maryland. We had no idea what we were to do.

During our travels, the close quarters with Caucasians on the train helped me see life differently from what I had believed was available to me.

Whereas they saw their future limited only by their talents, I saw mine as one that was allowed to flourish only by the whims of the white person in charge.

Our group was well educated and open-minded. They accepted me as one of them. As a result, my self-esteem grew stronger, and I began to feel more American.

CHAPTER 21
ARMY CHEMICAL CENTER

The Army bus met us at the train station in Baltimore. Finally, we learned where we are to be assigned. It was the Army Chemical Center. I am not sure if this bit of history I heard was accurate--that this camp was originally a cavalry base when horses were part of the military.

The facility was composed of permanent structures and had a nice recreation room with a fireplace and very comfortable chairs for relaxing. Our sleeping quarters were upstairs. It was not crowded, like the other camps, and we had the luxury of single beds. Next to our sleeping quarters was another recreation room. This is where the men spent most of their leisure time watching TV.

I went downstairs and walked into the main recreation room in the building. I noticed a very professional-looking slogan above the fire place. It read "*SEMPER PRIVITUS.*"

I looked at my friend Bill and asked,

Doesn't that say always privates?

It sure does, Bill answered.

The story was, a few years back, some of the men connived a joke on the officer in charge of the building. The officer did not know Latin, but he recognized "*SEMPER*" in the Marine slogan "*SEMPER FIDELIS.*" Not knowing any better, he approved the wording. Consequently, the sign above the fireplace. It said "*ALWAYS PRIVATES*," meaning no promotions.

We had top-secret clearance, but the captain in charge, a career soldier, had none. He had no idea what we were doing and could not go where we went. Every morning, he called reveille. We were to stand in formation before being dismissed for breakfast, but not everyone got out of bed. Those who didn't hung small signs on their beds that said "*SHIFT WORKER*." Our research work continued twenty-four hours a day; there were no shut downs, so, we had rotating shifts, day shift, swing shift, and night shift, there was no way the captain could keep track of our work schedules.

Three dogs slept in our dormitory. One of the fellows made sure they were fed. They roamed freely in and out of our sleeping quarters. One dog was named Black Dog, since he had black hair. The other was named Brown Dog, since he was brown, but the third was called Hogan.

Why did you guys give this dog a special name? I asked.

Oh! He was often at the base golf club chasing after the balls. So, we named him after the golf pro Ben Hogan, one guy answered.

The work site was some distance from our living quarters. Three lines of defense surrounded the building. Each was a high chain-link fence with one entry and a guard station. I had a badge with my photo on it, and as I walked past one station, I exchanged it for another badge of a different color with my photo. The badge at the last station was the one I wore in the building. Everyone working there wore the same color badge. We were told that all information on what we did or saw was not to be mentioned once we left the facility. The men observed this policy, and in the barracks, nothing was mentioned about our work.

Not much military decorum was practiced. No one seemed to mind who outranked whom; it was our particular skill that mattered. Our lives were professional at the work site, but normal and casual back at the barracks.

The cooks were not happy with us because when we were on the swing or graveyard shift, there was no way we could leave the site. So, they had to prepare sandwiches in brown bags for us. They resented the extra work.

One time, we had difficulties at the plant, so the engineers in another section were requested to give us the solution. Several years later, after we were back in civilian life, Andrew Cook, who I met when we were waiting at Fort Lee, became my very close friend. We were married and had children about the same ages. Andrew's wife liked Joy a lot, and we had dinner at each other's homes many times. One day, Andrew and I talked about the good times we had at the Chemical Center, but something bothered Andrew. He looked at me and spoke.

Rodney, remember when you guys sent over your problem to us for a solution? Andrew asked.

I was surprised to learn he was the one who received the problem to solve.

Yes! I didn't know you were the one who helped us, I said as I faced Andrew with a surprised look on my face.

Did my solution work? I kept calculating and recalculating, and each time I got the same answer. I knew something was wrong because the BTUs were extremely high, but I was under pressure. I had to send over my answer. I was sure there was an error some place, Andrew said worriedly.

Andrew, you were right on the button. It worked, I told him like I was proud of him.

What a relief for Andrew. When we were at the Chemical Center, there was no communication between the different sections. Top secret was maintained. He never knew the accuracy of his answer, until he and I, one evening, years later, while our wives were chatting together, talked about those days when we were young and in the Army.

CHAPTER 22

WEEKENDS AND TRIPS AWAY FROM THE BASE

When we arrived at the Chemical Center, we learned that the administrators had assigned us to wherever they could find an empty bed. So, we were broken up into smaller groups of about five more or less. The other men who had been there many months before we came treated us as outsiders. They had formed close relationships among themselves, and they shunned us. For the first time, I saw discrimination, not on racial lines but on strangers. Eventually, they tolerated us, and we slowly became good friends. We felt ignored but not isolated because there were enough of us from that train trip to enjoy camp life together. This experience helped me understand human nature in a broader sense.

One of the guys bought a used book titled something like this—"*Washington Exposed*." I don't remember exactly. However, the title did have the word" *exposed*" in it. Most of us had never been to Baltimore. One chapter in that book was devoted to Baltimore Street. That chapter drew our attention. Several guys wanted to get together and explore that street. I wondered why? I found out soon enough. That was where the bars with strip shows could be found. We used that book to find them. We were all in our early twenties. Watching any pretty girl would draw our full attention, especially when seeing her doing her dance routine, stripping and teasing the audience.

There were at least six of us. For a few of us, this was a first experience going to a bar. A couple of us never drank alcohol, not even a beer. Just as we entered the bar, a woman immediately started toward us. Then I noticed the bartender signal her to leave us alone. He knew we did not have money to spend. The stage was in the center of a horseshoe shaped bar where everyone sat and had their drinks while being entertained by the stripper doing her routine.

We had to buy a minimum of one drink to sit in for the show. So, we ordered beer, not only because we didn't know one mixed drink from another, but we didn't trust what the bartender might put in the drinks. Our budget only allowed us to sit in for two shows. We bought the minimum of one beer. So, after the first show, we went outside and sat on the sidewalk curb waiting for the next one to start. Can you imagine what we looked like sitting out there with nothing else better to do? I am sure we created quite a spectacle.

We were all in our early twenties and pushed by our hormones and curiosities. For me, it was more than the entertainment. I was part of a group of Caucasian guys just going through an innocent stage of life growing up. This was an illusion that gave me some assurance that I was not being judged by stereotyped preconceptions. It gave me a secure feeling that I was in a safe haven, shielded against any narrow judgment against hateful stares from strangers watching me.

Soon other weekend destinations occupied our interest. The guys had grown up aware of the many tourist attractions available. I knew only the few places where we felt comfortable visiting, places where we felt safe and less hostility. We never talked about those places we felt unwelcome in. They were just vacation sites others enjoyed, not where we would dare to go. Therefore, my knowledge of all those places was very limited. So, I just allowed the men to make the suggestions, and I joined them wherever they chose.

Bill and I met in the barracks at the Chemical Center. He was a chemist and worked in the chemical laboratory. The building where he worked was some place near us. I never knew exactly where. He never talked about his work, and I never asked. He grew up in Inglewood, a small suburb in Los Angeles County. We became very close friends that lasted past our Army career into our civilian life. Bill had his car at the Army camp, and on a few weekends, he and I went to see the various places close to Washington DC. One day, while we were in the recreation room, Bill mentioned he wanted to visit the Chateau Frontenac in Quebec, Canada. He invited us to join him and help pay for the travel expenses, including the cost for gasoline. We asked for and received a week's pass to make the trip. There were four of us, and Bill did all the driving.

First, we stopped in Portland, Maine, and visited a fish market. I saw lobsters with claws for the first time. Lobsters in California did not have claws. I bought four of them and paid to have them packaged alive and shipped to my parents back in Los Angeles. The next stop was Lincoln, Maine. What a beautiful town. We only had enough time to drive through for a quick sight-seeing tour before heading for Canada.

When we reached Canada, we stopped at a restaurant for lunch. The waitress gave us excellent service, and it seemed I got extra-large portions. One of the fellows started a conversation and found out she was married to the Chinese cook in the kitchen.

Oh! So that's why you got the larger portion! my friend said jokingly.

They then teased me and had a good laugh about it.

We were touring the grounds of the Chateau Frontenac; Stan came over to me laughing.

Hey! Rodney, I was standing by this group of European women tourists and overheard one of them exclaim, "What Japanese in the American Army already?" Stan said to me with a huge grin on his face.

This was 1953. World War II was still fresh in their minds as if it had just happened yesterday.

We followed the tour docent, a proud World War II veteran with wartime ribbons pinned on his shirt. This time, we were with a group of American tourists. One lady asked,

What is so special about this cannon?

It was a little shiny brass-plated cannon set on a concrete pedestal with a chain on four posts enclosing it.

We captured it from the United States during the war of 1812, he said with pride as he faced the women.

Then one lady turned toward us. All of us were in our uniforms and she spoke.

Well! Boys, what are you going to do about it?

Her timing was perfect. Everyone had a good laugh.

Traveling with my friends from camp protected me against any unpleasant attitude that might be against me. This freedom from fear allowed me to connect with all the beautiful features available for me to enjoy. For that moment, I felt I belonged.

CHAPTER 23

ARMY LIFE AS A
MARRIED COUPLE

I had been on the East Coast for over a year. During my stay there, I discovered so many interesting sites mentioned in travel literature. They were right there, within a short distance of where I was stationed. The water of Chesapeake Bay was just a short walking distance from our Barracks. New York City and Washington D.C. were less than a day's drive away. I could be enjoying all three locations with Joy if she had been there. I thought about this every time I went out with the guys sightseeing at the many tourist attractions near us. Finally, I made up my mind. Instead of waiting until I got out of the Army to marry, why not do it now? We may not have the time to travel the distance from California to vacation on the East Coast later on. So, I wrote to Joy.

Let's not wait until I complete my Army service. Why not marry now and live as a married couple? We can enjoy seeing the Eastern part of America together while I am stationed here.

There are so any interesting places near the Chemical Center, places we may not have time to visit after I return to civilian life. This is the perfect opportunity while I am in the Army, so close to the Blue Ridge Mountains. New England, Washington D.C.

Let's get married now.

She agreed. We were married the day before Washington's Birthday, February 21, 1954 at the Hollywood Beverly Christian Church in Hollywood, Los Angeles. She picked that day so I could remember our anniversary each year. As it turned out. I was so busy building a career that I could not remember whether we were married before or after Washington's birthday. She finally gave up and realized it was futile to expect that much from me.

Our trip by car back to the Army base from Los Angeles was our honeymoon. We visited every tourist trap along our route from Arizona to Florida, then up the Atlantic Coast to Baltimore. It was wonderful. As it turned out, we were right; there was no opportunity to travel to all these places later when we were raising our family.

We visited Carlsbad Caverns in New Mexico. Our timing was perfect. We ran into Mardi Gras in New Orleans. We didn't know it was being celebrated. Luckily, one motel had one vacancy. So, we were able to stay for a couple of days, not only to enjoy seeing people dressed in costumes, but to have dinner at the famous Court of Two Sisters. Then we drove up the coast of Florida, stopping at Silver Springs and Marineland. In Virginia, we toured Williamsburg. Finally, we arrived at the Chemical Center. As we drove toward the camp that late afternoon, a flock of Canadian geese were circling and landing on the Chesapeake Bay. What a pretty sight! So many birds loudly honking and landing in the water.

Our first two weeks were spent in a private room in the building for married couples. Joy got a taste of Army life living there and eating in the mess hall. Then I found a one-bedroom apartment with a kitchen and a bathroom just outside of the base. It was actually federal housing for underprivileged families. Many married Army couples lived there. The civilians living in that housing project were extremely poor; we saw children go into the garbage and pick out the watermelon rinds we had just tossed out. So, from then on, we tried not to do it in front of them. It was heart breaking for us. Reality struck home very hard when the lady next door asked if we could spare a stamp so she could send a letter to someone.

Joy had no means of transportation and knew no one. I didn't realize that she felt trapped with nowhere to go. I thought she could meet some of the neighbors. But it didn't happen. She was a little timid and not very outgoing. She was alone, lost, afraid, especially when I was on duty on the swing or graveyard shift. I imagine the evenings and night times during those times were hard on her. I didn't know her predicament until one day, by chance, I read a letter from her friend encouraging her to step out and make friends. That was when I learned how miserable she felt living in this federal housing project for the poor. I couldn't help. I had duties on the base.

I spoke with her after reading that letter. She told me how miserable she felt and jokingly said:

I was ready to divorce you and take everything you have.

Fat chance. We were just starting out. I had nothing of value, except my monthly Army salary and the car.

Eventually, Joy got to know the basic facilities, such as the PX. But what stood out the most was the post theater. The men had a way of enjoying the movies, even though some were not first-rate stories. I heard this mentioned quite often.

If the movies are bad, we laugh at it. If it's good, we laugh with it.

Joy and I decided to go to the movies one evening. The theater inside was the nosiest place on the base! Everyone was poking fun at the movie instead of enjoying it quietly. Joy had her first experience inside watching *"From Here to Eternity." We sat down hoping to enjoy the story, but there was so much noise in the theater, it was hard to hear the dialog. Prew was the key character played by Montgomery Cliff. In one scene. Prew said:*

Because I am a soldier.

Boo! Boo! shouted the audience.

They had no respect for military life. Joy stood up clapping her hands and shouted,

Hooray! Hooray for the Army!

Then she sat down and said to me with a smile,

Someone has to stand up for the Army.

We didn't have much money to spend, so she decided to save a dollar and give me a hair-cut. She had never done this before and several times lost control of the electric cutter. Boy! Was my head a mess. Her saving grace was the post barber. He was not the best. So, I blamed it on him.

Joy never had to budget her spending; her mother had done all the shopping. She was given a spending allowance and happily bought whatever she wanted. Once we were married and living off base, she had to do the shopping. It never occurred to her that food was an important part of the budget. Many times, she complained that I was stingy and wouldn't let her spend freely. So, I let her do whatever shopping she wanted. Then we came to the last week of the month. She had already spent the money, and no more was available for food. We had bullion soup and bread every night before payday. She learned her lesson. From that time on, she would squeeze a dime so tight you could hear it scream.

Our research project continued twenty-four hours a day with no shut down. We worked day, swing, and then graveyard shifts. The shifts rotated between us to allow everyone some change. It was hard on her being alone and knowing no one. She also had no means for traveling, except for a distant walk to the bus stop. She felt isolated with nothing to do.

A few months later, I received orders to go with a group of men to Alabama. Our assignment was to help a private contractor at Muscle Shoals in the northeast corner of Alabama solve a problem. They were under contract to maintain the facility at the ready.

We were in a separate building from the civilian workers at the plant. Everyone in our group was compensated for the expense of living off base.

I forgot where we stayed the first night. It must have been some local motel. Then, I found a vacancy in an apartment complex located in Sheffield. The town was one of the tri-cities that included Muscle Shoals and Florence. The apartment was furnished. Within a few days, I went to the newspaper office and bought a subscription for daily delivery. A lady greeted me and arranged for my newspaper service.

Come visit my family some time. Here is my address, she said.

I thanked her politely and left. Back in Los Angeles, this kind of remark was not serious, just casual saying with no real intent. So, I never went.

When my enlistment in the Army was coming to a close, and I had to return to the Chemical Center, I stopped by the newspaper office to cancel my subscription and pay whatever I owed. The same lady was there and scolded me politely for not visiting her family. I had not taken her invitation seriously because I was from Los Angeles. Things were different in Alabama; they said what they meant.

The lieutenant in charge of our group was worried about how I would be treated in the Deep South, but I was accepted like any white person. It seemed the people in the area just wanted separation from "*colored folks;*" they were treated very poorly. There would be two drinking fountains next to each other, one for "*whites*" the other for "*colored.*" The department stores provided a lunch counter for whites on one side and for colored on the other side. The lunch counter for colored folks had no seats. The public schools for Black students were easily identified because there were no fences surrounding the playgrounds. The theater ticket booth was in front of the building for white and in the rear for colored. Inside the theater, the main seating was downstairs and reserved for whites. The balcony above was for colored. As if that was not insulting enough, the front edge of the balcony had the typical three feet high protection wall, but in addition, it had a metal screen installed from the top of this wall to the ceiling. The screen was made of heavy gage metal with 2-inch diamond shaped holes to see through. Colored folks had to watch movies through this screen.

I was too young and naive to make judgements on the South. I was just glad they did not treat me this way. I felt a little insecure for fear the Southerners might also look down on me. But it did not happen. Asians were people they knew very little about. My presence among them made no impact on their way of life. So, other than being curious, they tolerated me as one of them.

However, a few of the men in my Army group did harbor a superior feeling towards me. I saw them as intelligent but immature. They came from the densely populated cities in the North. There were times when their attitude and degrading remarks were hard to take, but I managed because of one outstanding person, Calvin. Calvin came from the state of Washington. Several times he criticized me for the stereotyped beliefs I unconsciously had about white folks. I never realized I had those beliefs. They were ingrained in me as just a part of life. He tried to make me see the folly of being opinionated.

What I saw in Alabama brought back memories from the 1940's through the war years. Those were the days "white only" was on many property deeds in California. The real estate sales office's listing book of homes for sale said "white only". Civil Rights had not yet become an issue. Bigotry existed, and people looked down on minorities like in a caste system. I got caught up with this stereotyping in a very subtle way. I didn't know better. Our Chinese environment had divisions among the different spoken dialects. We knew how white folks looked down on the Okies. I remember one-time when I was in jr. high my Chinese friend said to me:

I am glad we are near the middle.
White people look down on Asians, Mexicans, and Blacks.

Asians look down on Mexicans and Blacks.
Mexicans look down on Blacks.
The Blacks have no one to look down on, so they are mad at all of us.

He said this in jest. It was really meant as a joking comment. But how truly he described human nature. Somehow, fate tossed all of us together in this unique land called America, where we are faced with a choice to survive in harmony or forever live-in turmoil. Perhaps being in the middle means being American. We're not perfect, but continuing to improve our behavior towards each other.

Joy's mother was a blue-eyed lady from Kansas City, Missouri. She had been a missionary in China and adopted Joy when she was a baby. When she heard that we were going to stay in Alabama for a few months, she telephoned Joy and warned her.

When you get to Alabama, remember you are not in Santa Monica. Do not wear shorts when you go shopping. Only colored people dress that way.

Joy learned to drive while we were in Sheffield. When she applied for a driver's license, the application called for race, so she wrote "*Chinese.*" The clerk looked at her answer and asked,

What's that?

Joy quickly scratched that out and wrote "*yellow*"

The clerk again asked,
What's that?

Then Joy wrote "*Mongolian*"

When that clerk asked the same question again, Joy just gave up and wrote "*white*." The clerk immediately issued her the driver's license.

Often, when I walked down the street, people would stare at me. It seemed like they had never seen an Asian before. But it didn't bother me. I returned the look to them and said with a smile,

How are you?

That broke the ice, and they would ask,

Where are you from?

I knew the answer they were looking for, but instead, I said,

California.

I think my humor caught them off guard, and soon we were relaxed and had a friendly chat. Then I told them I was Chinese, but several generations American, I made friends that way.

Joy and I had so much fun there. Wilson Dam on the Tennessee River was just outside of town, and we spent many evenings fishing off the banks behind the dam. I did not need a fishing license because I was in the military. But Joy was supposed to have one, so she used a drop line to fish, and whenever a warden appeared, the entire line was dropped into the water to avoid a citation.

One day, as we drove along the country road, she noticed some bushes growing wild along the road. They were loaded with plums, little ones no one bothered to pick, so we did and had the most delicious wild plums we'd ever eaten.

I was interested in Indian lore and would spend time going into plowed fields to hunt for arrowheads. I have a good collection of them even today. The locals thought I was crazy. They had seen so many relics that it was nothing special for them.

Many times, I would drive the dirt roads just to enjoy the simple country life. The first time I was driving on a dusty dirt road, a car behind me kept tailgating me. I tried to shake him off and couldn't. That evening, I told my neighbor in the apartment complex about it.

That guy tailgating me sure irritated me. He must have been trying to cause a fight, I spoke.

No, that is the way to drive on a dirt road to avoid eating the dust from your car, he replied.

After thinking it over, it sure made sense.

Summer was very hot, and in the evenings after supper, we would sit outside with the other tenants and have a grand time together. One evening, the conversation was about the drought and how cotton suffered from lack of rain. Someone mentioned that the area might have to get some federal money to help the farmers survive.

But the stream just outside of town was fed by a spring, and there was enough water to float a rowboat.

I said.

How deep is the ground water?

The city engineer lived downstairs below us and was part of the friendly gathering.

About fifty feet, he answered

I was dumfounded and said, *I bet I could run you folks out of the farming business by digging a well and not having to depend on rain.*

Oh no, you won't! the Engineer said.

Why not? I asked.

Because we would run you out of town before you could, the Engineer shouted.

Then everyone burst out laughing. It was a humorous evening. We enjoyed every bit of the friendliness.

I loved the local people. I was from Los Angeles, where life was, let's say *different*. Where else would this happen to me? I was looking for a particular item and asked the clerk if he had it. He led me to the door and pointed to his competitor and said,

I am sold out of it. But that store over there still has some.

Meanwhile, as our work continued at the chemical plant, I received orders to return to the center. My military commitment was reaching the end. While in the Army, I felt like I belonged. Especially, when I lived among the neighbors of that apartment complex in Sheffield, Alabama. Now, I was about to return to Southern California. How would I fit back in? I had seen and experienced life outside of my neighborhood culture. It had been like a breath of fresh air. Different. In my ethnic culture, we were very careful how we conducted ourselves because the white community was quick to judge us unfairly. But while I was among my Caucasian Army friends, I felt free to make mistakes and correct them, without being judged by narrow minded beliefs. I would be returning home to Southern California to rekindle old friendships and hope they would understand that my outlook on life had changed. I wanted to continue to enjoy myself, like when I was with my Army friends, but now without the shield of protection I got from being with them. I would be returning to Los Angeles, and I wanted to be myself and not be afraid of being unfairly stereotyped.

CHAPTER 24

THE MID 1950'S TO THE EARLY 1960'S

I had written a letter to L.A. County that I had completed my two years in the Army and wanted to return to the L. A. County Flood Control District. I had only worked there less than a year before being drafted into the military. On my first day back, I was assigned to work under Carl.

My initial experience working under his supervision was very discouraging. He wanted to hold me back so I would not be able to improve my skills and advance to higher positions. Carl motioned me with his finger to come to him.

Take these plans back to Fred in the file room, he demanded.

Other, new employees were given simple engineering tasks with samples to help guide and train. Carl, instead, treated me as an errand boy, not a trainee. *Have you ever had that uneasy feeling of not being wanted?* I felt that way. There I was, assigned to someone who believed that minorities belonged in "their place."

To Carl, that meant I should never rise above him. He did not have a college education, but had worked his way up through the ranks as an apprentice engineer. I admired that, but he saw me as someone who could someday advance past him. I was going to night school to earn another degree, this time in civil engineering. His engineering knowledge was limited. He had reached the peak of his upward mobility and would remain a senior engineer, but would never advance to a supervisory position. He lacked the knowledge required to pass the state license exam. I was going to evening school at USC, but needed the practical experience to qualify for the exam. He would not allow me to have the training other new employees received.

Carl sat at his drafting table by the window in the next row of tables. We were in a huge room of about 100 people, divided into squads of five to ten engineers and one or two draftsmen. A senior engineer who held a civil engineering license was in charge. Carl and I were just two of the many workers in that room.

My co-workers were congenial and friendly. They had unlimited opportunities. For me, there was a ceiling that was extremely difficult to break through. True. Civil Service exams are unbiased and fair, but the written exam was somewhere around 75% of the eligibility. The other percentage was called "*promotability*" and was determined by hierarchy. They used this tool to weed out those who could cause dissension among subordinates. However, it could also be used as an excuse to prevent minorities from reaching important positions.

The few that were from the Depression era were retiring and being replaced mostly by veterans from World War II. They had earned their engineering degrees under the GI Bill. I was one of the new ones, veterans from the Korean War. The supervisors in the county were mostly Caucasians, and we minorities traditionally held the lower positions. Our upward mobility was limited.

I see this period from the mid 1950's through the early 1960's as the beginning of the end of a culture dominated by a white hierarchy that would soon be challenged and forced to share with minorities. At that time, there was no open resentment towards a system that limited a minority on how far we could advance. It was an unspoken caste system. These were the years just before the pent-up anger would explode and begin to open the doors of opportunities to everyone. I am fortunate to have lived through this part of history because what happened from when the Watts riot occurred helped me become more tolerant. America was slowly awakening and realizing that perhaps our purpose on earth is to learn that all humans have feelings and rights, and we must not let greed overcome good behavior towards each other.

My position in the work place was tenuous. I could not aspire to goals a Caucasian took for granted. One bad remark uttered by one person was enough to justify a stereotypical belief against minorities. I had the uncomfortable feeling of not really belonging. I felt unwanted. I was left alone to fail.

But there were educational opportunities, and I had the GI Bill. I used it to attend USC in the evening while working during the day at the county and received my training academically instead of from the work place. I was determined to learn by continuing my studies in civil engineering. Eventually, I earned my Master's degree.

The friendliness among everyone, both the Caucasians and the minorities, was genuine at work, but after work, it was a different story. They lived in the newer tract homes. We were confined to older areas. This was a class distinction, and it made me determined to excel in my chosen career. I did it by staying alert and perceiving if I could have come up with better solution than they did in the jobs they were entrusted to but denied to me.

One day, I read a notice on the bulletin board looking for a teacher in civil engineering sponsored by the quasi-union for county workers. The teaching position was in the evening. I thought to myself. *This is one place where I could use what I learn in school and test my ability to reach for the sky.* So, I applied for it.

I thought it was a no-pay voluntary position in the county to help aspiring engineers improve their skills. To my surprise, it was a paid position in the junior college system at Metropolitan City College. I took the opportunity and taught lower division civil engineering. That position led me to teaching an evening class at East Los Angeles City College. Teaching was my most rewarding experience, and it helped me see solutions more clearly as I tried to explain the theory and application for practical use.

My Black co-workers stopped greeting me by my first name—they addressed me as Mr. Rodney or Mr. Chow. I was mystified.

What happened? Why did you stop calling me Rodney like old friends? I asked one of them.

You are a professor now. You are teaching in college, that fellow replied.

I didn't need any further explanation. They were showing me respect. I was very honored.

In the beginning, most of my students came from civil service offices. Then as time progressed, many came from private engineering offices. These were the ones who were working their way up in offices specializing in residential land development, and they wanted to earn a Bachelor's degree and eventually pass the state license exam to practice civil engineering. Many of my students were ex-GI's from the Korean War. Since I was too, this created warm relationships that extended beyond just teacher and student.

Two years later, when I passed the state exam and received my civil engineering license, my supervisor at the county gave me a valuable opportunity. He chose me to be part of a team writing engineering promotion exams, reviewing the correctness of their solutions and grading them.

The City of Los Angeles had a panel of practicing engineers who determined the promotability of newly licensed civil engineers applying for higher supervisory positions. My supervisor placed me on that panel. This valuable experience helped me see the other side of the decision-making process for selecting qualified employees.

Much later, another opportunity came. This time, it was from one of my students whose engineering office needed my expertise. The project was a huge land development in the desert. Every year, during the rainy season, water from the adjacent hills flows naturally unrestricted, but needs to be controlled. They needed an engineer who could help them solve the problem. A new direction for my future surfaced. It was like breathing fresh air! I began to have visions of private practice, but I needed a few more years of engineering experience before attempting that move.

Today, as I look back to those days of the late 50's through the 60's, I see myself at the cross roads of a new era. I found myself standing at a fork in the road, not knowing for sure which road to take. One choice was to play it safe and take the route that had proven safe for minorities. In other words, in the vernacular of the bigot, know my place and stay in it. That meant accepting my role as secondary to the white majority and not attempting to live in their neighborhood or trying to compete with them for important job opportunities. The other road was to take a chance, go into areas perceived as hostile to us and find out if we could coexist without creating fear that our presence would be detrimental to their wellbeing. A new era, a new generation, we were the new engines of growth and prosperity. People saw how my knowledge could add to their success and were willing to let me show I could fit in with them.

In 1969 in the eastern part of the Santa Clarita Valley in the towns of Aqua Dulce and Acton, I stumbled into a humble and friendly community, where down to earth and unpretentious people lived.

CHAPTER 25
BUYING MY FIRST HOME

The year was 1955. I had a secure job at the County with a comfortable monthly salary. Time to think ahead. Live the American dream—home ownership. That is what I wanted. To move away from the old neighborhood in the City Market area and find a nice house like my white co-workers had. There was a newer area known as the Crenshaw neighborhood. It was not in the suburbs where all the new subdivisions were being built, ones my people could not buy, although it was very close to where we lived in old houses among light industry, homes the original white community no longer wished to stay in. They still owned most of those houses, and we were their tenants.

Throughout my youth, I had heard about how we were prevented from buying houses in better neighborhoods. So, there I was, about to enter a hostile environment, to try to buy from those who believed my presence next door would bring down property values and hamper their good life. It was legal then to restrict neighborhoods to whites only. Shouldn't my service in the Army during the Korean War have earned my right to be treated equally?

I went to a real estate office in the Crenshaw area of Los Angeles. The agent spoke to me politely. But he said,

I can show you homes North of Jefferson Boulevard, but not South of it.

He didn't have to say any more. I knew just what he meant. I looked straight into his eye, with anger, totally silent and ready for a fight. He was standing about three feet in front of me, not a very tall person, maybe three or four inches taller than me. Then I hesitated, without a word, turned around and walked out of his office.

Joy and I had heard there were a few Asians living in the Crenshaw neighborhood. That was why we went there to look for a house. I told a friend about my experience at that realty office. He told me to go to a Japanese realty office in Little Tokyo. They might help us.

We did and were still upset about that episode as we spoke to a Japanese agent.

Last week, we walked into a real estate office to look for a home in the Crenshaw area to buy. The agent told us to stay north of Jefferson Boulevard and refused to show us houses we wanted to see. But I did see some Asians living there.

You walked into the wrong office. We know them—they are trying to keep that area white. There is one independent Japanese broker that has managed to get listings by convincing owners he has a list of financially strong Asians buyers that will pay premium prices. He can help you, he advised.

But by then, my attention was focused on Santa Monica and West Los Angeles. My wife and I were living in her mother's apartment in Santa Monica. We intended to have Joy's mother live with us. She was in her sixties, and we did not want her living alone. Back when Cammie was a young missionary in China, a turn of events occurred. She and her fiancé were to be married as soon as he returned home from the World War I in Europe. He would join her in China to do missionary work for their church. He had witnessed such terrible carnage in the battlefield and came to the conclusion that there is no God. If there was, God would have prevented this from happening.

Cammie told the Chinese pastor she refused to marry him because he had renounced his faith. When he heard this, he told Cammie,

China is not a country where you spend your life without family. My wife is pregnant, and we both want to give you our baby so you will have someone when you are old and retired.

The baby would have been their fourth child. Cammie was present for the birth. After the newborn had been washed and wrapped in a blanket, the pastor's wife, the natural mother handed her to Cammie. At that moment, on March, 8th, 1930, she became a member of the family. Cammie named the baby Joy Ruth Gray.

They lived across the street from the pastor's home, and the children were accustomed going in and out of both their home and Cammie's. To them, she was family. That was why there was no question about it—Cammie will not be left alone; she will live with us.

It may seem strange for Westerners to accept *"giving away a child."* Were they poor and unable to afford the child? Maybe they had too many children?

One has to understand the difference in customs between the West and China. Cammie lived among the villagers. She became one of them, helping them through the Christian Church where she served as a missionary. When she accepted the child, she became one of the family.

Another reason I wanted her to live with us was because during the war, when people were leaving ahead of the advancing Japanese army, she joined the refugees, pushing a wheel barrow with her little Chinee daughter in it. It took her one whole year to reach safety. She could have left on the last boat leaving China, but she chose to join the Chinese refugees because the officers on that ship insisted on a separation between White and Chinese. White folks occupied the cabins, and the Chinese had to stay below deck. Joy was just a child. She would not let them separate her from her daughter. So, she picked up Joy, walked off the ship and joined the refugees.

Cammie and Joy

We felt it would be good to buy close to where Cammie had friends and began visiting real estate offices in Santa Monica. But when we went there, no one came out to greet us. We sat waiting. No agents appeared. They were hiding. They did not want to help us. When we caught one sitting around waiting for a customer, the agent told us there were no homes available. This practice was completely in the open. The laws did not favor us. Neither did the courts. *"America is a free country."* They seemed to say, *"It is our right to discriminate as we choose."*

Some real estate agents wanted to sell to us, but were afraid the home-owners would stop doing busines with them should they sell to nonwhites. Joy's mother tried to help. They told Cammie if she was the fee owner, they could freely show us homes and sell to us. Cammie was mad and told them they had no reason to treat us that way and insisted we be treated fairly. Not everyone agreed with the real estate agents. We found one seller who had no preconceived attitudes and sold to us privately without an agent.

The next hurdle I experienced was the escrow officer at the bank. She gave me bare minimum service in a very cold and unfriendly manner. She asked me for my down payment, and I handed it to her. Without a word, she took the check, got up and immediately deposited it into the escrow account. I felt like I was not trusted, as if I would back out of the transaction at a moment's notice. Then she handed me some papers I couldn't understand and insisted I sign them. I did, but with the full intention of seeing my lawyer if I had been misled.

After all the paper work was done, I stood up, looked at her and said,

I do not like the way you treated me. You could have at least told me what the papers were for before insisting I sign them.

My voice was loud and filled with anger. The escrow office was at the end of the room where people were depositing their money. They heard me and turned their attention toward the escrow office.

The atmosphere in that office could have been more congenial had I known the function for escrow in a business transaction. I was 26 years old, unfamiliar with home buying. I felt she had a fiduciary responsibility to at least tell me what the papers were for. She could have been more helpful and treated me with a little more respect.

We moved into the neighborhood and noticed there were a few Asians living there. The houses were typical tract homes. But to me, coming from the old East Side of Los Angeles, it was paradise. I was living west of Bundy Drive and north of Olympic Blvd. I had no problems with the neighbors, and they treated us without prejudice. Most of us in the neighborhood were young couples, and many of the men were ex-GI's. I realized the unfriendly attitude that I experienced was mostly from the real estate agents. They felt they had a commitment to preserve property values by restricting home-ownership to whites only.

Those were the days when people envisioned a threat to their life style from cultures, they felt were inferior to theirs. It took just one minority in their midst to cause fear amongst them that their neighborhood would come crashing down. The realty agents who saw an opportunity to gain list-ings by telling homeowners to get out before their neighborhood lost value exaggerated their fears. It was a blockbusting propaganda that caused panic selling. Sad for everyone. Particularly for the minorities, because when white folks moved out, their economy left with them. The sudden outflow created a resentment among the minorities that fostered distrust between cultures. I felt that those unfortunate happenings prevented the minorities from smoothly assimilating into the American way of life. Fortunately, this did not happen to me. We became a part of their community naturally without having preconceived beliefs about each other because the few Asians living there had not changed their life style, and that paved the road of acceptance for us.

1955
The first home we purchased
1700 Amherst Street in West Los Angeles

CHAPTER 26
THE BEGINNING OF A NEW LIFE

My family began to grow. Bruce was first, then came Keith. Cammie was in heaven being grandma to the boys. Every waking hour was grandma time. The boys would sit on her lap while she read to them or played games with them.

Grandma was always happy to babysit the children. This allowed Joy to have a carefree life, and she didn't have to work like other wives. I had a Cal-Vet loan for the house, and the GI Bill provided enough cash to pay for college tuition and property taxes. My employment with the Los Angeles County Flood Control District provided a salary sufficient to provide a comfortable life for my family; my monthly payment on the Cal-Vet loan was $45 a month. My salary was $350 a month. Gasoline was twenty cents a gallon. I had a good life.

We lived just a few blocks away from the community called Sawtelle. I heard the city wanted to upgrade the neighborhood with new construction. They rezoned the area from single residential homes to multi-residential homes. At that time, one could buy a very old house in that neighborhood for about $4000. The contractors came, bought these houses, and replaced them with apartments.

I read a story about a young Jewish boy who went to the trainyard with a bucket to gather chunks of coal that dropped onto the train tracks. In winter, he would sell them door-to-door and was able to bring in extra cash to help his struggling family. I thought, the contractors couldn't possibly buy all the houses available in the market. The houses left were just like the chunks of coal that dropped on the train tracks.

I wanted to buy one house at a time and sell it to the contractors, just like that young boy did with the coal. I would buy a house and put it up for sale, while renting it out.

But the realtors were not willing to sell to minorities. Agents could discriminate against us; it was legal. Often, I was told to my face that they would not sell to me. I had just gotten out of the Army where they told us everyone was equal. Now, narrow-minded individuals for whom I had risked my life to preserve their freedom could deprive me of my freedom to live where I pleased?

I am not going to let them do this to me. I decided. *I am going to walk into an office, sit down and not give the agent a chance to speak until I've had my say. No! I won't threaten anyone, although I want to. Deep down, I really want to destroy their office piece by piece. But realistically, I will appeal to their desire to make money.*

So, I randomly picked a real estate office, walked in, and sat down in the chair in front of a desk. The agent was a middle-aged redhead with blue eyes. Then I boldly announced,

I want to buy and sell real estate in the Sawtelle neighborhood. If you are willing to do business with me, I promise no one will buy or sell for me but you.

There I was, a young twenty-eight-year-old Asian with a monthly income of only $350 talking like a big financier. She calmly sat in her chair and smiled and said,

I will.

From that moment on, a trusting relationship blossomed into a very close relationship. Ruth was the treasurer of the Beverly Hills/Westwood Realty Board. When she spotted a good buy in the listings, she immediately called me, and I would always say yes. She quickly told the other agents her client had purchased it and took it off the market pending close of escrow. After work and before I went home, I would go directly to her office and give her my check for the deposit. The next day, she'd call her loan officer to begin the purchase process. When the escrow had closed, Ruth placed a "*for rent*" sign on the front lawn and relisted the house at a higher price. We waited until a contractor made an offer, then sold the house for a profit.

I bought and sold one to two house per year and doubled my monthly income. This teamwork was possible not only because of the trust between us, but also because of my financial security in floating a loan.

Later, when her sister died and the family held the service the next day, I discovered Ruth was Jewish. Maybe it was her Jewish values that caused her to treat me so well. I could not have accomplished so much without her help.

One afternoon about 5 pm, Ruth came over to my home.

I want you to buy this house to live in. It just got listed, she said in a very serious manner.

Ruth, I haven't thought of moving. Where is this house? I said in a curious tone.

It is on the corner of Midvale and Ohio, just south of Wilshire Blvd, she replied.

I know that house. It is huge. I am not sure I want it; I spoke.

Now, you listen to your mother. Buy it! Ruth demanded.

I hesitated and thought about it. Near 8 in the evening, I called Ruth and spoke.

OK, I'll buy it.

She rushed over to my house, and by 10 pm, I'd completed the offer to buy at the asking price of $50,000, owner to finance. It was a good buy. I would be living in Westwood, a neighborhood I never dreamed I could move into. Ruth sold my old house for more than I paid for it. This gave me a healthy cushion financially. We moved into our new house, feeling a little worried. How would we be received? To our surprise, we were greeted with open arms. The lady across the street baked a pie and presented it to us as a welcome gift. I discovered Ruth had canvassed the neighborhood and told them I was a civil engineer and taught evening engineering classes at the college. Times had changed. Formerly silent ones were no longer afraid to speak up for us. Besides, I am part of that generation of Chinese who act like Americans. This created a comfortable atmosphere between me and my neighbors.

A few years later, Ruth came across a twenty-unit apartment building. It was located in the heart of Sherman Oaks, just north of Ventura Blvd. and a few blocks east of Sepulveda. It was an excellent location, but the economy was in a recession, and they were having difficulty selling this building. Ruth saw an investment opportunity for me and wanted me to have it. She came to my house and spoke.

Rodney! There is a buyer, and he is pounding the price so ridiculously low that it will be a huge loss to the seller. The seller is in trouble financially and has to sell. I hate to see him hurt so badly. I want you to offer $200,000. To buy it. This is a higher offer, and I am sure he will take it.

I know this is a good buy at that price, but I can only come up with $20,000. Cash. The bank will want more cash down before they will loan me the purchase money, I said worriedly.

Go ahead and make the offer. I will make it work, she said.

I bought that apartment building with a first trust deed, a second, and a third. That was a gamble. But I was just thirty-one years old, a little reckless and young. I had leveraged out the loan to the limit. It took me two years before I was able to make a profit from rentals by raising the rent allowed by the city rent control rules. From then on, each year's rental increase gave me spendable cash.

By then, I had become so comfortable with everyone outside my neighborhood that it never occurred to me, all my tenants were Caucasians. I had unconsciously become part of mainstream America. Besides, people had made great strides socially, and these tenants were not concerned that I was Asian. They only cared about the maintenance of the grounds and building and, of course, the rent.

It has been many years since I was an apartment owner. Since then, the older apartments were demolished and replaced with very desirable condominiums. My apartment building was one of the early ones sold to developers. The profit from these sales became the foundation for the business ventures I was about to enter into.

Going back to those days when I first became an apartment owner, I learned from that experience that the tenants were mainly interested in their comfort and life style. How the apartment was managed was extremely important to them. I did not cause any big changes in management, and there were no huge surprises for them. The one major change I did make though was as the younger tenants moved out, I chose the older retired ones by offering a reduced rental price only for seniors. I hired a handyman to come once a week to cater to the elderly and instructed him to do even the most mundane task to keep them happy and comfortable. A box was kept by the manager's door, and the tenants were instructed to place their written request into it for the handyman. He was told to keep the tenants satisfied. A gardener kept the landscape neat and vibrant, and an independent laundry service company was contracted to place coin-operated washers and dryers with very reasonable prices in the laundry room for tenant use. They profited, and I received a token income for my share of the laundry income.

What I learned back then was extremely important. The tenants accepted me as one of their kind if I did not cause any changes to their comfort level. My racial identity was not as important as how my presence affected their lives. They got to know me, and there was no mystery about me for them to fear. In retrospect, that contributed to my becoming less an ethnic curiosity to one being one of them, an American.

CHAPTER 27
YOUNG, INEXPERIENCED AND A BUDDING CAREER

It was 4:30 pm. Time to quit work. I had just one and a half hours to eat dinner and go to class. I wouldn't get home until 10 pm. This was my routine three days a week, Monday, Wednesday and Friday, the days I had class at USC. I had a Bachelor's degree in petroleum engineering. But I wanted to change over to civil engineering. There were more opportunities for me in that field.

I wasn't the only one sitting in class a little tired with red eyes. Most of my classmates, like me, were going to evening school under the GI bill. We had families, worked during the day and attended evening school.

Phillippe's on the corner of Alameda and Ord near the Union Station was where a group of us from the county bought our dinner before going to class. My favorite was a French dipped sandwich with delicious slice of roast pork, cole slaw, potato salad, and a can of Coca Cola. Once in a while, I would order a bowl of their delicious beef stew. Some of the guys bought a can of beer. I don't know how they stayed awake in class after drinking beer.

If I was still living in my ethnic neighborhood, I would be living very close to USC and would have stopped at home for dinner before going to class. But I lived near Santa Monica, at least an hour drive away from USC, just like the others who lived in the other direction eastward in the newer subdivisions. Every one of us who stopped at Phillipe's were there for the same reason. We needed a quick dinner before going to class, and stopping at Phillipe's with all the guys from the county brought me closer to them and made me feel I belonged.

Back in the office, two or three times a year, someone would announce a new addition to his family. He would go desk to desk passing out cigars with a sign; it is a baby boy! Or a girl! We were the younger ones, filing the gaps as the older engineers began to retire.

Then another time someone bought a new car.

Wow! Let's us go look at it.

That was the consensus of most of the young engineers in the office. As the years passed,

It was Congratulations, you passed the EIT.

This was the air of anticipation and excitement as each young trainee engineer advanced in his career.

The EIT was the state-qualifying exam to evaluate our knowledge of four years of college engineering classes. Passing this exam allowed us to take the civil engineer's state license exam after we had two years of experience under a licensed civil engineer. We were the next wave of licensed civil engineers.

Those were the highlights for me back in the late 1950's through the early 1960's. Although there was a ceiling in Civil Service as to how far I could advance, I was able to live with it as something beyond my control because Civil Service employment was secure and pay was comparable to similar positions in the private sector. Also, the coworker's friendliness made me feel like I was one of them. The secure employment made it possible for me to easily qualify for loans to buy and sell real estate for profit.

While some of the men invested in stocks, I was more interested in buying and selling real estate. This gave me an insight into private enterprise. There was no ceiling there, and I concluded that this was one avenue where I would be able to succeed to the fullest of my ability. This was in contrast to Civil Service where I was just tolerated by those in charge. There were two different scenarios. Only one would allow me to feel wanted and assimilate fully as an American. I was beginning to see that my future would be in the private sector.

CHAPTER 28
FAMILY LIFE

*C*ammie, my mother-in-law, lived with us. It was not always a smooth relationship. She had a hard time adjusting to not being the head of the family.

I am 5' 2", and she was about that height as well, but she outweighed me by fifty pounds. I'm telling you, when she got mad, I felt like a World War II Sherman tank was about to run me down.

Cammie had spent her early life as a missionary and a church leader in Wuhu, China. She was accustomed to being in a leadership role, so there were occasional disagreements as to who ruled in my home. She came from a well-educated Southern family in Kansas City, Missouri, and in China, she had lived among the elite Chinese from universities. I came from the east-side of Los Angeles where every day was a struggle to survive. The families I knew were gradually learning American ways, despite being strongly tied to the old ways of the villages in China. But the Army influenced me. My colleagues were all college educated men from white families. So, I was not a total stranger to the modern ways of America.

Nevertheless, she'd say to me,

That's not the way we do it in America.

I tried to conduct myself the way she felt was proper. Then she came around the corner and surprised me by saying,

That's not the way we do it in our part of China.

Get it? **Our** part of China?

Well, she had lived in Northern China, and I am a descendant from the South. There's a saying among the Northerners about us Cantonese Chinese from the South. *"They eat anything with four legs except the table, but two will do, like frogs."*

Anyway, we had a mutual respect for each other. I loved her. She was my children's grandmother.

Joy loved animals. Our house was on a corner lot 150 feet long and fifty feet wide. A fence across the middle of the backyard separated the well-land-scaped portion from the rear area, where the clothesline and the incinerator for burning trash were located. We never bothered to maintain that portion of the yard. It was full of weeds. An alternate gate could be used to enter directly from the side adjacent to the street. I built a walk-in cage ten feet deep by six feet high stretching across the rear. We raised chickens and other birds as pets for the children to enjoy. It seemed like every child on our street was in our yard playing every day. I built a tree house over the peach tree, and it became their playhouse. The tall weeds were perfect for the children to play in and crawl through on their bellies.

Normally, neighbors would complain about a messy yard and especially our rooster crowing in the morning. But every family had a child who loved to play in our yard. One boy was so engrossed playing that he never stopped to go home to take a pee, and at the end of the day, he went home in wet pants. One day, I saw this same boy with a baby chick cupped in his hands, rocking back and forth, singing *"rock-a-bye baby on the tree top."* What a treat it was watching him.

I dumped a pile of dirt about six feet high in the middle of that yard, and the children dug tunnels and created roads on a make-believe mountain for toy cars. They were happy and covered with dirt. At the day's end, Joy would have our boys stand outside on the grass as she washed them down with the garden hose, then stripped off their clothes before letting them into the house. I wondered what the other mothers did with their happy, dirty children when they got home.

Joan lived on the next block from us. She loved to play in our yard with the other children. She was a cute young girl. Then, one day she surprised me. A boy pushed her aside, and she came after him with a toy shovel in hand, yelling,

God dammit, Johnny!

Hey! Hold on there a second young lady, I said to myself. That is a mighty tough little girl.

When we bought a new car, we made sure it had vinyl upholstery. When children are in a car for long drives, accidents happen. Nothing to get excited about, when we got home, we just opened all the doors and hosed down the insides.

Our son Bruce, wanted to be a Cub Scout. He joined the group in his elementary school. So, Joy and I took him to the department store and purchased his uniform. He tried dressing in it and saw himself in the dressing room mirror.

How does it fit? the sales person asked.

It looked great on him.

We will take it, Joy said

I saw the proud look on his face. He insisted on keeping the uniform on all day.

Joy became a den mother, and our home was where the boys met. She met the other mothers and became part of the community.

When the Cub Scouts graduated to Boy Scouts, I participated with the fathers in sponsoring and assisting the boys in their scout activities. I became part of the community of fathers that kept our neighborhood together. The men were from all different levels of income and work. Our interest in creating a healthy experience for the children brought us together. I became assistant Scoutmaster, and other fathers and I took the boys on scout camp trips. The boys slept in their tents, and several of the fathers slept in sleeping bags outside or in the back of their station wagons.

I bought a family sized tent to sleep in. When the fathers saw it, I got outvoted, and my tent was confiscated and happily made into the community poker room. While the children slept quietly, you could see the dim light from outside and hear the loud laughing as we fathers played poker inside the tent.

When I was my children's age, my parents had finally emerged from the Great Depression. However, they were still tied to the old ways of Chinatown. Not quite American, yet different from their parents who still held onto the old ways brought over from China. My parents built the foundation for pride and a self-esteem that enabled me to become a part of the community in West Los Angeles where I bought my first house on Amherst Street. My children grew up among Asian, Mexican, and Caucasian children.

Just like my parents did for me, I did for my children. I encouraged them to excel in school and reminded them that they must not ever do anything that could disgrace the family. I believe that is the foundation I instilled in them for their success as they entered their adult life. Most importantly, like my parents and their parents, as each generation became more familiar with American ways, we did not abandon our moral values as we provided them a home that was more American than the one, we came from. I gave them the foundation to believe without a doubt that they are American.

The Sawtelle area had a small community of Japanese, or actually, two communities. One was centered around the Methodist Church, and the other, the Buddhist Temple. I met and became friends with them. The ones I knew best were from the Methodist Church, were of my age group, and veterans from the Korean War. Some were gardeners, while others were professionals with college degrees.

Some of the Japanese men collected and polished semiprecious stones. This was new to me; I never thought of appreciating stones that way. I became interested in the hobby and started to attend free exhibits of the different rock hound clubs and saw their beautiful displays of polished stones and cuttings. I particularly liked the petrified wood. Those were the days when that hobby was very popular. Mom and Pop stores sold equipment for cutting and polishing agates, jasper, etc., and rough uncut semiprecious rocks could be found any place we traveled in the United States.

We had a Volkswagen camper, and each year, we explored places I never dreamed I would visit. That was the era of the hippies; we were enjoying life just like them and were slowly losing our fear of being mistreated or unwanted.

One year, we vacationed at Gold Beach in Southern Oregon. What a wonderful place away from the city! We walked along the beach and noticed pebbles in the water. That reminded us of the beautiful stones we saw in the club exhibits. We searched and searched, but couldn't find any as pretty as those in the free shows. We didn't know they do not become like that naturally—they have to be polished.

Slowly, we were emerging from the cocoon of our ethnic environment and were becoming part of the new age of young Americans.

Some of the Chinese families I grew up with in our segregated neighborhood came from homes more adventurous, and they traveled to places like the national parks. But my parents had been struggling to survive the Depression and worked seven days a week to just scrape by. Even after they became successful, they could not change their ways and enjoy going on vacations. So, I did not have those opportunities in my youth. Traveling and visiting places everyone took for granted with my family was a huge learning experience for me.

Our most memorable trip was to Crater Lake in Oregon. Joy and I saw pumice stones for sale in the gift shop.

Wow! Let's buy one, we said to each other, so we did.

Then as we drove out of the park, we saw pumice strewn all over the place.

I became fascinated with my newfound hobby and got together with neighbors to start a rock hound club. One of the Japanese men was a geologist and part of the faculty at UCLA. He helped us. He led our field trips to hunt for jasper agates and petrified palm roots.

Soon, we went on rock hounding trips by ourselves. We went as far as Utah in the Northwest, Wyoming in the East, and New Mexico in the South. There was a camaraderie among rock hounds. We would start out alone in our Volkswagen bus and meet other rock hounds on the way. Before we knew it, we'd joined up with them as if we had known each other forever. It was several days of friendly companionship. I felt very comfortable with these down-to-earth people, just learning to appreciate them by being myself was just one of them enjoying the desert away from the city. We did not stand out as different.

The Volkswagen bus was light and didn't get stuck sinking into mud, so we recklessly crossed creeks and muddy portions of dirt paths by going full speed through places where some drove four wheelers. It was fun. Joy and the boys just hung on for dear life as I floored the gas pedal and sped over some poor excuse for a road.

I particularly liked going to the desert side of Oregon and Washington and attending large events where tailgaters sold polished or raw materials to hobbyists. The organizers, many times the Chamber of Commerce, would have field trips to lead us to where deposits of good material could be found.

Somehow, the thought of being Chinese-American never crossed my mind. I never felt like an outsider amongst them. I had become one of them.

I didn't know it then, but this hobby soon led me to where I would build my private practice as a civil engineer.

CHAPTER 29
STARTING MY
PRIVATE PRACTICE

A l said to me,

Rodney! You are American as apple pie.

His comment came right out of the blue. I was unprepared for it. There had been no real important conversations between us. We were co-workers at the Los Angeles County Flood Control District, and I was passing my responsibilities over to him. He said it so casually, the words just came out as from one friend to another. It was like someone saying: "*You're OK pal.*" But for me, it was a milestone. That is how so many like me have always wanted to be viewed.

The office was planning a farewell party for me. I had given notice to county that I was leaving Civil Service to begin my private practice as a consulting civil engineer.

That was the beginning of a new life and career for me. It had only been about ten years since the thought of leaving a secure position in Civil Service was unthinkable. Attitudes had changed, and I didn't realize it until I decided to take a chance by leaving the county to look for opportunities in fields where most minorities felt unwelcome. To my surprise, there were many landowners waiting for an engineer to help them turn their property into spendable cash. They were only interested in whether I could help. Who I was did not concern them!

Times had changed, and I didn't know it til I gave life a try. Actually, it was not so much a change as it was an adjustment in comfort level.

Running an office was not just solving problems for clients. I learned that public relations are a must, and they don't teach that in the school of engineering. Some of our crucial problems came from those who thought they knew how our job should be done. One client hired us to set his lot boundaries. We had done several surveys for his developments, but this time it was his home. The survey crew was accustomed to just going out and doing the job. On construction sites, each subcontractor was expected to appear and start work immediately. There was no need to explain to the job foreman, unless it was something unusual. So, when Bob arrived to do the survey, he began measuring the entire block to establish the line from where he could set the lot corners. The wife of my client did not see the men working until they were in front of her home. When they received our bill, she complained that we cheated on the hours worked. His wife said the men only worked half the hours we claimed. She said she knew exactly how long they were in front of their home. We had to explain things, and he understood. But this was a lesson: Before beginning an assignment, make sure whoever hires us knows what it takes to do the job, and most important, ask him to let his wife know.

Another time, my secretary received a call from some lady complaining that our surveyor was using the instrument to look at her instead of doing his work. I sure didn't want to begin with a bad reputation. I turned towards my principal surveyor:

Go talk to this lady. Tell her our man was sighting a target to take measurements. He was not looking at her.

Later that afternoon, Rick came back to the office with a big smile on his face.

Did you talk to that lady? I asked him.

Rick replied. ***Yes! I was prepared to tell her that Bob was sighting through his instrument to make measurements, and he was not looking at her. I walked up to her door, rang her door bell and waited until she came out. You should have seen her! She was beautiful, dressed to kill. One look at her, and I forgot every word I had planned to say. I just blurted out, Wow! If my man was looking at you, I wouldn't blame him one bit. I got control of myself and started to tell her Bob was only doing his job. She was flattered, and before I could say any more, she invited me in for coffee.***

Back in the early 1970's, when I first thought of opening an office, I wasn't sure where my business would come from. It was a trial and error process. I started visiting local architects.

I worried about when the next job would come. Soon a trickle of new customers appeared. I discovered they were referred to me by another engineering office that couldn't take any more business. I didn't know the owner, never met him. But he thought of me and gave me a break. At that time, I learned how professionals conduct business. I also learned to keep clients away from my workers; clients tended to socialize with my men and attempted to get free information for which they would ordinarily be charged a consulting fee.

My business grew, and I was concentrating on small builders in the San Fernando Valley. Then one day, I began to notice the Santa Clarita Valley in the northern part of Los Angeles County. That part of the county appealed to me because large developers had not yet began building new subdivisions there. It was largely rural with ranches and open fields of vacant land. One or two engineering offices were established there, but I felt there was enough demand for engineering services for me to fit in. The question was *where can I find out about the people and learn what are their needs? Who do I contact to find those who are thinking about developing their land for a higher use?*

I drove through the valley and saw real estate offices that specialized in land. I visited them and found my contacts. It was they who held listings of vacant land, and they needed to know where the boundaries were located. I found a new source for expanding my business. My office evolved from doing small developments in the city to parcels measured in acres. That was a less crowded field of opportunity for small civil engineering companies. I had found my niche.

My friends from the old neighborhood wondered how I was able to establish a business where they had always felt minorities were not welcome. I had no problems, and that particular fear never entered my mind. I was an engineer, and I had a skill they needed. My ethnic background was not an issue. More important was making a friendly visit now and then, and I'd slowly become accepted as one of them. Other offices had a sales person bringing in business, but I was my own sales person. I wanted to "own" my clients and not leave it to a sales person who could someday walk away to another office with my clients.

The Fair Housing Act opened many areas to minorities. I could go anywhere I chose, enter a real estate office and not feel uncomfortable. My field of opportunities widened. I decided to look into areas outside of my neighborhood and discovered real estate offices that specialized in land. These offices became the key to my success. They needed an engineer and I was available. My success was possible because two surveyors, Rick Grant and Bob Klessert, helped me build my business.

Rick was a licensed land surveyor with many years of experience in the office as well as in the field. Bob was a land surveyor with many years of working with Rick; he did not have a license. Both of them have since retired. I lost touch with Rick, but Bob stayed in touch with me until one day his daughter called and told me he had died. I miss them. They were true friends.

In the meantime, my family grew from just two boys to adding a daughter, Carolyn. Our social life continued to revolve around our rock hound friends in West Los Angeles. We spent many weekends with them going to the Mojave Desert east of Barstow looking for petrified palm roots. Our Volkswagen bus had a built-in icebox with a small washbasin and water reservoir. We had so much fun gliding right along the highway with a tail wind, but driving against the wind was very slow.

I bought a rock saw with an 18-inch diameter diamond tip blade and a tumbler for polishing small, gravel size rocks. You should see my beautiful display of polished bookends and polished petrified tree logs of two to eighteen-inch-long tree trunks.

Each time we drove through the Santa Clarita Valley to go to the Mojave Desert, we passed by a little sleepy town just before Palmdale. That town fascinated me. I loved the picturesque setting. It reminded me of a small town with a deserted lonely street in a Western movie. As I looked down the street, I saw the whole town from North to South and pictured a tumbleweed blowing from one side of the street to the other and a small dog nonchalantly trotting across on a diagonal to reach the other side. It felt like living a moment in paradise, but we never had time to stop and visit. There wasn't enough time, and the trip to the Mojave was a long drive.

Finally, on one trip home from the desert, my curiosity took over. I turned off the highway and drove slowly down Crown Valley Road. The main street stretched from Sierra Highway in the North of town to Soledad Canyon Road in the South. That was the length of the town, just a few miles. I felt I could belong here. So, I stopped my Volkswagen to enjoy the scenery.

Unsuspectingly, this side trip was the beginning of a new direction for my career.

CHAPTER 30
TOWN OF ACTON

I drove slowly down Crown Valley Road. It must have been about 4:00 pm. Gosh! I loved what I saw.

Let's stop and go into that land office and chat with someone, I said as I turned to Joy.

OK! she answered.

We entered the office and walked toward the agent sitting at his desk. I greeted him with a hello and started a conversation.

Hi! I just happened to drive through here on my way home. What is the name of this town? I asked.

Acton. Where are you from? he asked.

Los Angeles. We've been on an outing to the desert. We love it out here, I mentioned.

What do you do? he asked.

I am a civil engineer. I just started my private practice. Every time we drive by on Sierra Highway, we notice this town. We were just curious and wanted to talk to someone about it, I replied.

A civil engineer? Do we need one! Seems few engineers are willing to come here because we are too small, and they cannot make much money with us. If you come and help us, we will give you our business, the agent said excitedly.

I jumped at the opportunity. Earlier, about a year ago, I had opened my office in the San Fernando Valley. It was close to my home in Westwood.

Jim was the agent I talked to. Later, I discovered he owned the land office. He gave me my start in Acton. The land was typical desert acreage with very little vegetation. Some lots were bought and sold without corner monuments to show where property lines were located. This was the high desert where parcels were two to fifty acres or larger. He wanted to be able to show buyers exactly where the boundaries lay. Many times, this required a land survey. Some parcels had homes on them, but property lines were still not easy to identify. Other times, he had clients with large parcels that could be subdivided into smaller acreages and sold separately. They needed a licensed civil engineer to help them.

When I met Jim, I had no idea it would be my start in land development, a specialty in civil engineering. I stumbled into a niche. Jim opened the door for me. He spread the word around town, and the townspeople gave me the support I needed.

I arrived in Acton when they needed an engineer. No one cared who I was. They only wanted someone to help them develop their land and increase its value. I was available. I love the people in this part of the valley. They are down to earth and unpretentious country folks.

One Saturday morning, I had just parked my car when I heard someone talking about a shooting at a popular local bar.

What happened? I asked.

Oh! This guy was at the bar when a bunch of motorcycle riders came in and pushed an old man aside to make space. He didn't like it when he saw that. So, he pulled out his gun and threatened them. They grabbed his gun and before you know it, he was shot with his own gun. He ended up in the hospital, but survived.

Who is this fellow? I probed.

Jason.

You mean Jason Brown? I exclaimed!

Yep, he confirmed.

Why! I was doing something for him on his land; he was my client. For a city boy like me, just starting to know this town, this incident was a colorful and exciting introduction.

My first challenging project in town came through Jim from the land office. Some time ago, he had sold this large parcel to an investor from Los Angeles. The investor was thinking of selling it. Jim suggested he hire me to split his land into four smaller parcels so he could sell it easier for a profit. So, he introduced me to him.

Jake, this is Rodney. He is a licensed civil engineer, and he can help you divide your land.

He hired me, and I drove out with him to see his property. It was land-locked but had an easement over the adjacent property for access to the public street. As we drove over the dirt driveway, a young boy flagged me down.

My dad wants to talk to you, the boy said.

I didn't think much of it and waited. Then a fellow with a rifle in hand came up to me and placed the tip of his rifle barrel right against my head.

I don't like strangers driving over my property, the boy's father threatened.

I looked at Jake from the corner of my eyes. Have you ever seen how white a White man looks white from fear? I had to think fast. I had no time to be scared. I reached into my shirt pocket, took out my business card and handed it to him and said,

If you ever need help on your property, give me a call.

It took him by surprise, and before he was able to think about it, I floored my gas pedal and drove out like greased lightning. As soon as I reached the street, I turned to Jake.

Next time you want my service, please let your neighbor know who you are before we drive over the easement.

Sometime later, Bill contacted me. He owned the other land office down the road from Jim's office. Jim had told him about me. Bill became an important part of my career in Acton. We became close friends.

Bill was a large person with the kind of personality portrayed on the TV series *"Bonanza."* Whenever I thought of him, I imagined Bill walking down Crown Valley Road with his three sons, just like Ben Cartwright and his sons in "Bonanza."

Bill knew a widow, Carol, living alone on 200 hundred acres. She told Bill she might sell off part of her land and wanted to know how to do it, so Bill told her to contact me. Bob, one of my surveyors, and I went to see her. When we were in Carol's home, she insisted we tell her our full names and birthdays before discussing business. I didn't think much of it; neither did Bob, and we gave her the information. It turned out she believed in numerology. That was the first time I heard of that belief. She had a system where each letter of the alphabet had a number. Then she wrote down all the numbers corresponding to the spelling of our full name and added it to the numbers from our birthdays. Mine came up very high. From that time on, I was very special to her.

I liked this lady very much, and since she treated me so well, I would always pay her a visit, sometimes bringing her a small box of See's chocolate.

Carol was an amazing elderly person. You should have seen how she drove—like a teenager, going full speed through the streets.

It turned out there was little I could do for her. But I remained friendly with her for many years.

Bill was a descendant of early settlers in town, and he knew most of the landowners. He wanted to subdivide and build ranchettes. He had one or two Arabian show horses, and consequently, knew what horse fanciers needed. He also knew Al and his partner, custom homebuilders. Bill was familiar with the homes they built, especially how they meticulously attended to details. He particularly noticed they were honest and reliable. I had the engineering knowledge to make a subdivision possible, and Bill had the land office and license to sell real estate. Together, we formed an informal partnership with a handshake to do land developments.

Bill knew of an old subdivision that had been recorded in the county many years ago but was never built. He told Al and his partner to check with the county to see if the lots in that subdivision were still legal. They were! Bill's strategy was very simple. Combine several lots together to create a parcel of at least one acre.

So, we got together to submit plans to the Building and Safety Department and received permits to build on eleven parcels. None of us had ever built subdivisions before. We were not sure how our venture would turn out. Bill would do the selling, and I would take care of the engineering. The economy was in a slight recession, and we figured that the first house might not sell. We agreed to draw straws. Whoever got the short straw would have to buy that house and parcel to take out the construction loan.

The first house was built, and Bill placed his "for sale" sign in front and waited. It sold within the first week! We thought maybe it was one person who happened by looking to buy, and he liked what he saw. So, we decided to get started on the next house and hope for the best.

The next week after the sale of that first house, the buyer placed a "for sale by owner" sign on the front of his new purchase. Now, that took a lot of guts to compete with us by putting up a for sale sign within our subdivision. And at a higher price!

He sold it in less than a week.

What is going on? we asked ourselves.

Then, as our backhoe tractor operator was digging out the trench for the next house, someone came, placed the second house in escrow, pending completion of the construction.

We had anticipated that it would take a few weeks or even a month after some advertising to attract a buyer. We didn't know it was the beginning of a housing boom.

I believe our original asking price was $55,000, but that first buyer sold his house for much more, so we decided to raise our price and profited beyond our wildest dreams.

I saw a future in building small subdivisions. The land development business attracted my attention. Instead of relying on others to keep my office busy, my engineering company concentrated on my own projects.

Maybe it was just luck. Others in the same business did not seem to encounter the opportunities that came through my door. Perhaps they were only interested in building up a reputable engineering company and did not want to be distracted from that goal. But I was always interested in the production end of land development. My successes evolved from my relationships with clients who asked me to joint venture with them.

My clients were not the companies that built hundreds of homes a year. Most were startups that took a parcel, subdivided it into four or more lots and built custom homes on them. We were beginners, each with our particular specialty, and we trusted one another. I grew with them, as they took on larger land development projects. Their budget could not afford an in-house engineering and planning staff. I was a start-up consulting office with a tight budget. Like them, I was willing to take the financial risk. It was a compatible relationship where we needed each other.

Somehow, my being an Asian and they being Caucasians never crossed our minds. We were the same age, financially comfortable with one objective-- land development. It happened many years ago. We were in our early forties, sharing the same ambition for success, and we became friends that fit together like family.

Michael was another person who befriended me. He and his partner came into my office one day. They needed some input from an engineer on a project they had. They were not sure whether I could be the engineer for them. Well, OK! I didn't mind talking.

Do you have a particular project you would like to discuss? I asked.

We have a parcel of land in escrow. We are looking for an engineer to help us upgrade this land to a design we have in mind, so we can sell it to a developer, Michael responded.

Where is this land located? Did you bring in any drawings to show me? I asked.

Yes, our parcel is located in the Newhall area in North Los Angeles County. I am an architect, and these are the renderings of the houses I'd like to design. The parcel could hold thirty-seven of these estate-type homes on large lots. We could make this a very desirable section of town, selling to high-income buyers, Sam, Michael's partner, said with pride.

I looked at the drawings. The homes he had drawn would fit nicely in the more expensive areas south of SR14 freeway in Iron, Sand, or Placerita Canyon, but not where they held this parcel in escrow. I told them their design was not compatible with current development and was too small to influence the existing trend in that area. It was over-designed and doomed to failure.

They kept in contact with me, but never engaged me to be their engineer. They spent two years talking to developers. Everyone told them the same thing. The plan was a loser. Finally, Michael convinced his partner to hire me and listen to my proposal. I told them I wanted to redo their entire concept and build a subdivision that would have the luxuries of a high-priced neighborhood but would sell at a price to meet the budget of the first-time homeowner. I could do this by applying the one-lot condominium concept, but with free-standing single-family homes on a restricted easement for each homeowner to maintain privacy. They were willing to give my suggestion a try and hired me. I was to complete all work necessary to obtain a tentative tract map, which included the conditions all the county departments demanded, before they would give their approval for the project. This is known as a paper subdivision. The approved tentative map meant a builder could build with confidence that as long as they worked within those county conditions, permits for construction would be issued. This increased the value of their raw land to one for a higher use, and they were able to sell it for a profit.

It was just before Christmas; they had made a huge profit from the sale. Michael called me.

Rodney, I want you to come to our office.

Why? It is Christmas. I want to enjoy the holiday. Can't it wait til after New Year? I asked.

No! You have to come to our office, Michael demanded.

So, I went, hoping to get it over with and return home as soon as possible. I walked through their door. Michael and his partner greeted me with smiles. Then he handed me a check for my fees and an extra $25,000. They sure staged a surprise for me. That extra money was great, but to me nothing could compare to their gesture of gratitude. I felt like I was walking on a cloud.

A few days after New Year's Day, Michael asked me to form a partnership with him to do a paper subdivision. I would do the engineering, and he would do the business end. We became friends, and that friendship introduced me to a very intimate part of Jewish life. I was invited to his daughter's Bat Mitzvah. It was an Orthodox ceremony. The men sat on one side and the women on the other. While we were waiting for the ceremony to begin, the men and women made fun of each other, saying which section was better. I enjoyed the human side of these people. When Michael invited me to come, I felt honored. It was another valuable experience for me along the road towards being American. I learned that people are the same, despite the differences between our cultures and back grounds. This was another opportunity that helped me expand my social skills with Americans I hadn't been familiar with before.

I had no idea I would someday get this far socially and in business when I started my private practice. The doors opened before me, and I walked through them.

When I had stopped to see the town of Acton and met new friends, I had no inkling that it was the start of a new direction for my career. It exposed me to a future I least expected.

CHAPTER 31
CARPINTERIA, CALIFORNIA

I had my sights set on expanding into Tehachapi to build ranchettes, and from there, going into the Bakersfield area. My vision for the southerly San Joaquin Valley was to create "orchards" of hundreds of acres on a condominium concept of ten acres sites. The orchards would be owned by an association of each ten-acre owners, but managed under contract to an agricultural organization. The buyers of each site would be from some large metropolitan area, city dwellers wanting a country getaway.

While I had been busy building my career, my wife, Joy, enjoyed a carefree life. She took care of our home, and when the children were about seven or eight years old, she took them to our local park to learn to swim. She met other mothers who brought their children to the swimming pool. The park manager got these young mothers together and started a tennis club. They became friends and expanded their social life, traveling together to tennis tournaments. I was in the same stage in my career as the husbands of these young women. We were very busy building our businesses and had comfortable enough incomes to allow the young wives to play tennis and vacation together as far as Europe without their husbands.

One day, one of the ladies mentioned her ex-husband had been trying to sell their five acres in Carpinteria. We were not familiar with the Santa Barbara area, but, just out of curiosity, Joy wanted to have a look. The reason it was difficult to sell was because the land was undeveloped and could only be financed by the seller. They wanted out and were waiting for a cash buyer.

We drove out to Carpinteria, stood on that piece of land, saw the ocean in front and the Los Padres Mountains behind. It took just five minutes to decide. We bought it. It was the perfect place for us to retire. So, we sold our house in Westwood, Los Angeles. Our plans were to build a nice house and enjoy a bucolic lifestyle. But the recession hit in 1988. I was building a 14 lot ranchette subdivision in the Antelope Valley and a four-building apartment complex in Palmdale. Suddenly, the market disappeared. I saw incomplete subdivisions by other land developers, some with concrete slab foundations completed and abandoned. My subdivision was completed, but I had not begun to build any houses. The bank knew I could not survive financially, so they offered me an opportunity to let them have my project and a $300,000 cash settlement in lieu of foreclosure. My brothers and sisters came to the rescue and helped me with a portion of the cash settlement. I stopped construction of the apartment complex and accepted the situation as the best option for peace of mind, free of all financial debts. The end of the housing boom arrived. I abandoned the construction of my six thousand square foot house and settled for an old, used, single mobile home. However, I did complete building a tennis court for Joy. We still had this piece of heaven with an ocean view and the beautiful Los Padres mountains behind.

The help I received from my brothers and sisters showed me the importance of family. When everything fails, family is ready to help.

We initially planned to landscape the five acres into a luxury estate, but reality sunk in, and common sense told us to utilize the land for farming. A new direction for me was on the horizon.

CHAPTER 32
A NEW BEGINNING

We came to the Carpinteria Valley to live away from city life. We would start anew, this time till the earth, live the simple life and become farmers. I knew very little about farming, but thought starting an orchard would be exciting. I wanted to grow something different than what was being grown here. Avocados and orchids predominated. So, I chose instead to start an apple orchard. Some people told me:

You should plant avocados; this is not apple country!

I saw apple trees successfully grown in some of the yards in Carpinteria. Of course, it was possible. I attended agricultural trade shows and made contact with sales people who knew the farm business. I read the available literature for growing apples and proceeded from there. It worked.

I planted Fuji together with Gala apples because they pollinated each other to produce good tasting apples. My land began to look like an orchard. We moved from Westwood, Los Angeles, a very nice neighborhood, but nothing as pleasant as the wide-open space of country living. Every day, we saw the train travel across the front of the beach. Some days, we could hear the ocean waves. No smog to worry about, the air was clean and refreshing. In the morning, the crows would fly across our farm, going towards Santa Barbara. Then in the evening, they were flying home to the Easterly edge of Carpinteria Valley. We looked up towards the sky and saw red tail hawks circling, looking for their next meal. Squirrels were munching on our fruit. Gosh! How could we save our apples? During certain times in the year, migratory birds flew across the sky. They landed on our farm.

Some had yellow breasts, almost like canaries. At night, we heard the owls hoot in the dark. Often, late in the night, the coyotes howled under our window. We heard them but we did not go out, because we did not want to scare them away.

I wanted our farm to have an identity, a name neither Asian nor Western Americana, something that could stand out as unique in the Santa Barbara County. Then we received some good news. Our son and his wife wanted a child but couldn't conceive one. They heard that the Holt Foundation had an orphanage in China that had just found a baby left in a basket in the market square. She was found on a bright day in Spring.

So, the orphanage gave her the name Bright Spring. They immediately had all the necessary paper work done for receiving the baby, then went to China to adopt her. We were so happy to have a granddaughter, so we named the farm **"BRIGHT SPRING RANCH."**

Rodney and Joy
Carpinteria, California

Joy and Rodney
Our apple trees in bloom

CHAPTER 33
OXNARD CALIFORNIA

I retired from engineering and became a farmer. I learned to send leaf samples to an agriculture laboratory to have them analyzed and received information for supplying the proper nutrients to maintain healthy trees. I also learned to send samples of leaves that were damaged by insects to an insectarium where the entomologist examined the problem and sent me the eggs of the beneficial insects to eat the pest.

Just nurturing fruit trees was not enough to keep me busy. I was 60 years old, still very active, feeling young and needing something to keep me occupied. What could I do with myself? I had bought and sold homes through a real estate broker and made money doing it. Just before retiring from engineering practice, I had partnered with one or two clients building ranchettes for sale. It would be natural for me to become a real estate sales person. I knew and understood title insurance, escrow procedures, fee titles, and what buyers wanted. So, I attended a class to learn what is needed to get a real estate sales license.

My first opportunity after receiving my license to sell was in a broker's office in Oxnard, Ca. This experience helped me understand the young first-time home buyer who wanted home ownership but knew very little on how to buy. It also informed me on how to find customers in an extremely crowded field. Selling certainly was not what I thought it would be. I had to convince the would-be buyer that I was a trusted sales person who could help find them a home they want. I was the new kid on the block, unknown, inexperienced and naïve. On top of all these impediments, Oxnard was a community mostly of Whites and Hispanics. There were very few Asians. The only way to find buyers that would buy or sell through me was to go walk the streets, knock on doors, introduce myself and let them know who I was. That took perseverance, a tough skin that could take rejection in stride, and a personality to sooth over irate people exasperated by so many agents trying to sell their homes.

Despite all these hurdles, I found some very interesting moments that livened up the job. Everyone had to spend time in the front office to answer telephone calls and walk-ins that were curious about homes in the area. The most interesting moments came from unsophisticated young persons that had always been renters and wanted to either find another rental or buy their first home, or just to pay their rent on rentals managed by our office.

One day while I sat on the front office, the telephone rang. I gave the usual greeting hoping it would be a potential customer. Then I heard this frantic voice:

Are you there, are you there?

The caller caught me in a good mood. I knew what he meant but, in that moment, I shouted back in a jovial manner.

I answered the phone, didn't I?

He came in late, afraid he might have to pay a cash penalty. The rental contract specifically said rent was due by 5:00 PM on the payment date or a $50.00 penalty would have to be paid. He was a low-income farm laborer, and every dime was important for his financial survival. I let him off the hook.

Another time when It was my turn to sit on the front desk, a young lady called on our advertisement for rentals. She wanted to know if the rental was an apartment or a condominium. Obviously, she did not know the correct pronouncement for condo.

Is it a condom? she asked.

I tried not to embarrass her by correcting her by saying that the rental was a condo, not a condom. So, with my utmost diplomacy, I said:

Yes, it is a condo.

Maria walked into our office. She wanted to buy a home. They had been trying to buy one but each time after finding one and writing a check for the deposit, they learned after a month that the lender refused them because their income could not support the upkeep and mortgage payments. None of the real estate offices they visited were able to help. Her husband had given up. He came with her only because she insisted. When I spoke with them, her husband sat looking disinterested. They had been rejected too many times.

I learned that they had a newborn baby and were living in a garage that had been illegally converted into living quarters. They slept and cooked in that one room. I told them there was a possibility I could help through a federal grant for first-time low-income home buyers. But they had to have good credit.

The federal government had a program to help potential buyers like them. it was a zero interest twenty-five thousand dollars government loan that had no monthly payments. That sounded too good to be true. The other agents had never mentioned this. They did not know, nor were they interested in the extra work. It was a second trust deed against the property that was recorded, and someday, if they sold that house, the money had to be returned.

This offset the sales price of the home enough for them to qualify with their income. I knew a loan officer from a community bank that was familiar with the program. They were willing to reduce their fees to help. With that help, the young couple had barely enough money to complete escrow.

I found a very small two-bedroom house for sale on the eastside of Oxnard. The interior needed much work, but met the minimum requirements for an FHA loan. The price was right. Most potential buyers would not bother looking into this messy property. I told them,

Make a low offer. You have the skills to make the improvements yourself. This is your opportunity to move out of the garage and own a home.

They did, and right up to the signing of the necessary papers in the escrow office of the bank, the husband seemed disinterested. He was expecting a rejection and did not want another disappointment. I looked at him and said:

Juan, we made it. The bank will give you the loan. You can now close escrow. You are going to become homeowners. Sign the papers.

Maria signed. Up to that moment, he could not believe it. He wrote his signature on the papers. The escrow closed. They became home owners.

Several weeks later, I received a phone call from Maria. She wanted to take me out to lunch. I hesitated. Then I realized she wanted to show me her appreciation. This kind gesture would give her a complete happy closure. I accepted.

That evening, when I came home, I told my wife about how Maria with her baby sat with me in the Hometown Buffet. I told her I felt like I was having pheasant on a silver platter. It was the best lunch I ever had.

Oxnard had a profound effect on me. I fell in love with the Hispanic people. They reminded me of my people when I was in my youth, like the Asians on San Pedro Street back then. They struggled and provided their families with a good home. No work was too low for them. They took whatever was available and worked hard. Many, despite their low wages, sent a portion home to Mexico to feed those they left behind. I remember that was exactly the path my people took back in the early years of my childhood.

Today, as I drive through parts of Santa Barbara, past the local parks and the Hispanic neighborhoods. I often see barbecue parties, colorful balloons floating in the air and held down by string, children playing excitingly, while women are sitting together organizing the picnic and the men either do barbecuing or enjoying each other with a can of beer. When I see this as I drive by, I wondered who really has the good life. Those living in palatial homes or these common folks with family. I understand why deep in our hearts, we enjoy stories of the simple life we know as Americana.

CHAPTER 34
THE GOOD LIFE

Initially, we gave our apples to friends and relatives. As the trees matured, it became urgent to find a way to unload the bountiful harvest. So, I joined the Farmers Market in Summerland, just a few minutes from our farm. That market was new and did not attract enough customers to support the few participating farmers. It closed within a few months; so, I joined the one in Ojai. That was the beginning of a new life for me. I met people who were friendly and down to earth. There were times when it was rainy and business was slow; these Ojai people would deliberately buy something just to help the farmers survive. They were the good people, country folks. They came to buy the fresh vegetables, fruits and flowers grown by the many young farmers who grew healthy vegetables without using any toxic sprays to control pests. But more than just shopping, it was where friends met and socialized. I had a new experience meeting people who cared about protecting the Earth for future generations.

We had no experience in selling. Our greatest difficulty was pricing. Many times, we sold below our breakeven point, until we learned how much to sell for a profit. I remember the first week. We didn't have much to sell and brought in a gross of $25.00. Wow! Let's go and celebrate. We spent $40.00 for dinner at a local restaurant. Now, just a minute. Is that how to run a business? Sure, we were happy to sell something. But better yet, why not bring more to the market and look like real farmers instead of someone who is growing in our back yard.

Joy came with me to help sell our apples each Sunday at the Ojai Market. During the week, while I took care of the apple trees, she joined a group of women tennis players in Santa Barbara and played tennis two to three days a week. Other days, she spent part of the day having lunch with her new friends or took walks with them.

Within a few years, I joined the Santa Barbara Certified Farmers Market. Reality soon dawned on us. Farming is serious business. We learned that it was more than just a place for locals to buy farm fresh products. It was also a place where friends meet. For me, it was a place where I met the local people, chatted with them and found new friends. They especially appreciated local farmers and would buy from them before patronizing farmers from another area. I found it refreshing when customers would greet me by my first name. It made me feel I belonged. Farmers Market brought me close to everyone from Ojai to Carpinteria and Santa Barbara. I would not have gotten to know so many throughout the County if I hadn't been part of Farmers Market. Like those from Ojai, these Santa Barbara and Carpinteria citizens are down to earth. I could not tell the common laborers from the professionals. No one cared. I felt comfortable among them. I knew they accepted me as a friend because they liked me.

It has been a long journey. My entire lifetime. Beginning way back when I was a child, as a minority shunned by the majority and looked down on unwanted, over my lifetime from those early 1930's to the present. My attitude has evolved along with so many as each new generation demanded changes in social behavior. It was this younger generation, the outspoken ones who sided with justice, that awakened us to how important it is to give others a chance. But more than that. It is to the Civil Rights Movement I owe a great gratitude, because they sacrificed their livelihood, endangered themselves against violence, and gradually won a place for equal treatment. It was this effort that opened the doors for me so I can say I am an American.

Many years have passed, and I now feel I am as American as anyone. It has been a journey that has taken me a lifetime. I succeeded by concentrating on the good and not dwelling on the bad.

CHAPTER 35
EPILOGUE

America was much different back in 1929, the year I was born. I grew up during times when well-defined boundaries prevented minorities from reaching the good life. Later, I experienced those years when changes in attitudes towards each other began to improve life. Those changes affected me as I began to realize that America could not continue to be a vibrant nation if we did not recognize and allow the talents of everyone to contribute to our nation.

When I left the Army, my goal was to rise in the ranks of Civil Service and retire comfortably with a pension. My belief was that my future would be limited by a culture which would not allow me to reach my full potential, that the glass ceiling created by the establishment could not be shattered. But as I matured, I became more open minded towards others. It took courage and a belief in myself to reach out, take chances, and become a part of building a better place for everyone.

I wrote this story of my life to let my readers understand my experiences as a minority. At times, it was hard, but not as bad as some may think. All that was needed was a willingness to go out and meet others from different backgrounds and discover:

We are all a part of a family known as Americans.